Negative Capability

POETS ON POETRY

David Lehman, General Editor
Donald Hall, Founding Editor

New titles

Tess Gallagher, *Soul Barnacles*
Linda Gregerson, *Negative Capability*
Larry Levis, *The Gazer Within*
William Matthews, *The Poetry Blues*
Charles Simic, *A Fly in the Soup*

Recently published

Rachel Hadas, *Merrill, Cavafy, Poems, and Dreams*
Yusef Komunyakaa, *Blue Notes*
Philip Larkin, *Required Writing*
Alicia Suskin Ostriker, *Dancing at the Devil's Party*
Ron Padgett, *The Straight Line*

Also available are collections by

A. R. Ammons, Robert Bly, Philip Booth, Marianne Boruch,
Hayden Carruth, Fred Chappell, Amy Clampitt, Tom Clark,
Douglas Crase, Robert Creeley, Donald Davie, Peter Davison,
Tess Gallagher, Suzanne Gardinier, Allen Grossman, Thom Gunn,
John Haines, Donald Hall, Joy Harjo, Robert Hayden,
Edward Hirsch, Daniel Hoffman, Jonathan Holden,
John Hollander, Andrew Hudgins, Josephine Jacobsen,
Weldon Kees, Galway Kinnell, Mary Kinzie, Kenneth Koch,
John Koethe, Richard Kostelanetz, Maxine Kumin, Martin
Lammon (editor), David Lehman, Philip Levine, John Logan,
William Logan, William Matthews, William Meredith, Jane Miller,
Carol Muske, Geoffrey O'Brien, Gregory Orr, Marge Piercy,
Anne Sexton, Charles Simic, Louis Simpson, William Stafford,
Anne Stevenson, May Swenson, James Tate, Richard Tillinghast,
Diane Wakoski, C. K. Williams, Alan Williamson, Charles Wright,
and James Wright

Linda Gregerson

Negative Capability

CONTEMPORARY AMERICAN
POETRY

Ann Arbor

THE UNIVERSITY OF MICHIGAN PRESS

2004   2003   2002   2001   4   3   2   1

A CIP catalog record for this book is available from the British Library.

Library of Congress Cataloging-in-Publication Data

Gregerson, Linda.
   Negative capability : contemporary American poetry / Linda
Gregerson.
      p.   cm. — (Poets on poetry)
   ISBN 0-472-09777-6 (cloth : alk. paper) — ISBN 0-472-06777-X
(pbk. : alk. paper)
   1. American poetry—20th century—History and criticism.
I. Title.   II. Series.
PS323.5 .G74   2001
811'.509—dc21   2001001401

Acknowledgments

The essays in the present volume were written over a number of years, in time stolen from other projects. I am grateful to the editors who prompted them and have given me permission to reprint them here: to Don Bruckner, Joanne Feit Diehl, Matthew Gilbert, Herbert Leibowitz, David Lynn, and, above all, Joseph Parisi. The map of American poetry presented in these pages is highly fragmentary, patched together in the usual manner of one who writes on assignment: one part editorial urging and one part accident for every third part of prior affinity. Many of the poets I most admire and consider most central to our common enterprise receive no mention here at all. Nevertheless, the cross-section seems to me a felicitous and a worthy one, more varied than I might have assembled on my own, resistant to easy generalization. I have learned a great deal from the poets represented here; their work has been a gift to me. As has the conversation of my friends and colleagues in poetry: David Baker, George Bornstein, Sharon Bryan, Peter Davison, Alice Fulton, Lawrence Goldstein, Jorie Graham, Marjorie Levinson, Thomas Lynch, Yopie Prins, Keith Taylor, Rosanna Warren, Patricia Yaeger. Steven Mullaney's is still the crucial judgment.

Contents

Introduction

Not long ago, a distinguished British editor, himself a poet, told my students what he thought of the poetry currently being written in the United States. There were exceptions to his general disdain, but they were few and in the end less interesting than the brute reminder of just how wide a gulf the North Atlantic can be, whether one takes its measure in verse or in the common forms of courtesy. Some of his assessments I will readily concede: failed poetry is plentiful on our side, as in any given time and place; the chronic varieties of failure (a fallback reliance on autobiography and "self-expression," for instance) have much to reveal about us. But the truer measure, I would argue, is that which is always more difficult to account for: the genuine achievements of thought and craft, the suppler expansions and refinements of idiom. Men and women of widely divergent cultural backgrounds, aesthetic persuasions, skepticisms, and registers of voice have produced in recent decades an American lyric of unprecedented variety and abundance. This lyric is rich, to my mind, in discipline as well as depth. That so much of it should be lost on those with whom we share a language (my British colleague spoke for many in his country) is telling but not mysterious: the incomprehension betokens a genuine bifurcation in poetic practice. There are, of course, salient differences between American and British sensibilities in other literary fields as well—in fiction, for instance, and in criticism—but there are also substantial commonalities in these two realms: we are generally still equipped to read one another's work. In poetry we might almost be on different planets. And the altered, the American, tradition has yet to be fully described.

The sources of this altered tradition may be traced to shared and venerable quarrels. One of the earliest essays in this volume took its title from an oft-cited phrase in Keats. I was trying to describe a characteristic presentational strategy in the poetry of Mark Strand, a calculated staging of the self as absent, unembellished by the adjectival clutter of time and place. I meant the phrase—*negative capability* transported from the realm of high Romantic theory to the ironized realm of contemporary rhetoric—to register as cheeky. But cheeky doesn't age well, and I find I meant the phrase more earnestly than I had imagined. Not that Keats would necessarily approve. He championed in the writer a "passive and receptive" posture and opposed this to a mode he called the "egotistical sublime"; Strand's wit (and that of other compatriots we might name) lies precisely in the conflation of these two poles, something on the order of a "passive egotistical." Keats rejected poetry "that has a palpable design on us"; this palpable design has modulated, I would argue, into one of the great semantic and tonal resources of contemporary American poetry, most palpably when it stages its own undoing. Keats praised the Man of Achievement (above all, the exemplary poet) for his freedom from the "irritable reaching after fact and reason"; the poetry, the American achievement, I wish to praise may not be long on fact and reason of the sort Keats had in mind, but it is filled with irritable reaching, as were, I might add, the Shakespearean poems Keats so admired.[1] These qualities—the performative rhetoric, the fractured self-consciousness, the irritable surface, the reaching—are at once the symptoms of cognitive method and the lineaments of form.

Form in the strong sense is not "received"; it is invented. Form is not the dead hand but the living measure of tradition. And, despite recurrent accusations, form has not gone missing from American poetry. Nor has it been sequestered in "formalism," old or new. Form has modulated in multiple, and often extravagant, directions, but the formal imperative of most consequence in contemporary American poetry has a single, recognizable center: one must learn something new in the course of writing the poem. That is to say, the medium itself must be mined for its insights, the language used in all its material reality as an instrument for inquiry. To report in a poem on what one has learned or felt elsewhere, to paraphrase some other mode of being, to end where one began: these are the hallmarks of *formal* insufficiency. One enters a poem to be changed. These strictures are hard to adhere to; they may be hard to distinguish from nearly plausible imitations. But even traditional templates may be reinhabited as though they were strange and new: see, for instance, William Meredith's extraordinary reinvention of the sonnet or Gjertrud Schnackenberg's reenchantment of rhyme. Multiple pitches of diction and voice may be played for hypertophic extension or syncopated overlay to yield a moral or a cognitive anatomy: see the very different talking lines of James Schuyler and C. K. Williams; see the fierce vernaculars in Muriel Rukeyser and Philip Levine; see Heather McHugh's back-talk, John Ashbery's urban riff. Image may lend a governing logic: see Jane Kenyon; see Mark Strand. The momentums of argument may be used with as much detachment, and as deftly, as if they were anapests and tetrameters: see Louise Glück. The now-collusive-now-adversarial contours of syntax and line may generate a music of consummate subtlety: see Glück again. All of these—rhyme and rhythm, diction and voice, the image made to work as argument, argument made to work as pacing or dynamic, the modulated tensions between one phrasal unit and another—all are the elements of form, and all may be used as ways of putting the question.

One set of fashions put us badly off the track, for a time, and seems to betray a peculiarly American dysfunction. The issue was gender, the decade was the long 1980s, and the message (a composite of writerly practice, readerly expectation, and editorial vogue) was decidedly mixed. Write, said America to its women poets, but write as ingenues. In poems as elsewhere we want you young: willing to simulate youth even as you age, willing to cultivate a freshness impervious to experience. Abstraction, sinew, complex syntax, breadth of historical and cultural reference—these are not for you. The successes of the ingenuous female voice in this period were notable—some of them are considered in the following pages—but the restrictive patronage of ingenuousness was unfriendly to women and writing alike. This unhappy narrowing has not disappeared completely (its roots are too much with us), but it is blessedly less dominant than it was.

As are, I believe, our worst oversimplifications about the relation between poetic discipline and poetic subject. Form is part of the poet's contract with time. The gestures of autobiography are part of the poet's contract with her reader and with form. When the American lyric is charged with formlessness it tends to be charged with unfiltered confessionalism as well. We have had, it is true, much to answer for here—a good forty years of on-again, off-again overreaction. But the stagings of personal voice and of personal attachment could not be loosely indulged forever nor lightly banished for long, however strong the recoil, and I think we've come to read and write with better balance again. There are reasons, often abstract or chiefly musical reasons, to plot a poem around the ostensible transparencies of personal history. The reader, for instance, may be asked to perform very difficult interpretive labors if she is offered an occasional resting place, where the poem appears to ground itself in the given or the poet to reveal her stakes in the poem. The linear workings of imagination may benefit from disruption by the inconvenient actual. The self invented to speak the poem, invented *by* the poem it speaks, may lend proportion and differential weight and an organizing center to vistas that would otherwise be too raucous or too flat. Can inductive method and personal voice serve as pretexts for self-indulgence? Emphatically yes. But so can the most impeccable formulas of prosody and genre. Poets weary of false oppositions (and falser yokings) have begun to restore the speaking self to its proper function as a structural and semantic resource.

Strong writing will always be rarer than the other kind. The writing of one's immediate contemporaries will always be hard to assess. Or, rather, it will be so if one is lucky and lives in a lucky time. I am, I believe; I do.

NOTE

1. All citations are taken from *The Letters of John Keats,* ed. Maurice Buxton Forman, 4th ed. (London: Oxford University Press, 1952). "Negative capability" and "the irritable reaching after fact and reason," from a letter to George and Thomas Keats, 21 December 1817. "Passive and receptive," from a letter to John Hamilton Reynolds, 19 February 1818. "Egotistical sublime," from a letter to Richard Woodhouse, 27 October 1818. "Poetry that has a palpable design upon us," from a letter to John Hamilton Reynolds, 3 February 1818.

1

Negative Capability

It seems to me that we should rather
be the flower than the bee.
—John Keats to J. H. Reynolds,
February 19, 1818

When Mark Strand reinvented the poem, he began by leaving out the world. The self he invented to star in the poems went on with the work of divestment: it jettisoned place, it jettisoned fellows, it jettisoned all distinguishing physical marks, save beauty alone. It was never impeded by personality. Nor was this radical renunciation to be confused with modesty, or asceticism. The self had designs on a readership, and a consummate gift for the musical phrase:

> I give up my eyes which are glass eggs.
> I give up my tongue.
> I give up my mouth which is the constant dream of my
>   tongue.
> I give up my throat which is the sleeve of my voice.
> I give up my heart which is a burning apple.
> I give up my lungs which are trees that have never seen the
>   moon.
> I give up my smell which is that of a stone traveling through
>   rain.
> I give up my hands which are ten wishes.
> I give up my arms which have wanted to leave me anyway.
> I give up my legs which are lovers only at night.
> I give up my buttocks which are the moons of childhood.
> I give up my penis which whispers encouragement to my
>   thighs.
> I give up my clothes which are walls that blow in the wind
> and I give up the ghost that lives in them.

First published in *Parnassus: Poetry in Review* 9, no. 2 (1981): 90–114.

I give up. I give up.
And you will have none of it because already I am beginning
again without anything.

("Giving Myself Up")

The poet's career has thrived on the honey of absence, and,
mid-career, Mark Strand has come forth with *Selected Poems.* The
overview is both impressive and timely. Beneath a changing
prosody, the central poetic strategies exhibit remarkable coher-
ence. On the stage it had cleared, the self divided itself for dia-
logue: the I became an I and a you, an I and a mailman, an I and
an engineer; the face appeared on both sides of a mirror, both
sides of a picture window, both sides of the printed page. In
1978, with the simultaneous publication of *The Late Hour* and *The
Monument,* the divided persona became a divided corpus. *The
Monument,* a prose collage, is the logical extension of all that
went before it: here the poet divests himself of even his poems.
In *The Late Hour,* conversely, and surely as a consequence, the
banished populations begin to reassemble: place names, per-
sonal names, the items of use and the trappings of memory re-
sume some luster of their own. The habitual and strategic re-
nunciation that characterized the earlier poems has been
siphoned off into an extrapoetic territory. The new poems, those
in the last third of *The Late Hour* and those that complete the pres-
ent volume, have thus been freed for the work of restoration.

1.

In the *Selected Poems,* the first polished surface held forth for re-
gard is a series of ingenious couplets, the title poem of Strand's
first book:

> Unmoved by what the wind does,
> The windows
> Are not rattled, nor do the various
> Areas
> Of the house make their usual racket—
> Creak at
> The joints, trusses and studs.

("Sleeping with One Eye Open")

This urbane series of feminine rhymes and triple rhymes and slant rhymes culminates in no less than a version of analyzed rhyme; the echo must multiply to complete its variations, and the couplet expands to become a final triplet:

> And I lie sleeping with one eye open,
> Hoping
> That nothing, nothing will happen.

Open, hoping, nothing, happen: the rhyme sequence constitutes, among other things, a witty portrait of paranoia, wherein the most feared eventuality is most devoutly invoked. The passive verbs or verbals (*unmoved, rattled*) activate an echo of another sort. These words are the commonplaces of psychological portraiture; context and tone suggest that we construe them as such. But their grammatical subjects (*windows, areas*) argue for a purely material interpretation. Thus two semantic frameworks are poised in sympathy and competition. Irony is hardly an adequate term for tactics of the sort this poem deploys.

There are antecedents. Prosody, at least, has been refined to this particular double edge before, and Strand undoubtedly studied something of tone from Donald Justice, whose perfect elegance is always perfectly double. Justice has polished a surface in order to aggravate the discrepancies between manner and tone, has cultivated, in other words, the inherent ambiguity of perfect manners. His powers of inflection are subtle in the extreme, and nowhere so subtle as when he merges the cunning and the apparently ingenuous, as when, for example, he would have us encounter death in an end-stopped couplet. A chasm opens beneath the studied naïveté in Justice's evocation of a grandmother's funeral:

> I remember the soprano
> Fanning herself at the piano,
>
> And the preacher looming large
> Above me in his dark blue serge.
>
> My shoes brought in a smell of clay
> To mingle with the faint sachet
>
> Of flowers sweating in their vases.
> A stranger showed us to our places.
>
> ("First Death")

This poem is in fact a poem of middle age. Though Justice is the senior practitioner and was for a year Strand's teacher, it rather behooves us to discuss affinity between the two than to track down primogeniture. Strand quickly cleared ground of his own and made the reciprocities of influence one of his primary themes. In their volumes of mid-career, Justice and Strand entertain a sporadic dialogue in which homage is sometimes difficult to distinguish from exorcism, the dialogue of journeymen who have learned one another's lessons well.

For a brief time Strand's prosody assumed more flamboyance than Justice's ever has, but the virtuosity was quickly toned down and channeled in other directions. The surface complexities of Strand's first book afford considerable delight, though rhyme and meter and wordplay occasionally leave plain sense and syntax to fend somewhat for themselves. At times humble denotation puts up a thin resistance to flashier connotation. Now and again, the poems exhibit imperfect tact, as any young poet who speaks too knowingly of "Old People on the Nursing Home Porch" is likely to exhibit imperfect tact. But the poet's informing preoccupations are already full-blown. When, in the same first volume, Strand's poems emerge with the simpler surface we think of as characteristic, dislocation is still a central mode. The world and the self appear to exist ever more at one another's expense:

> In a field
> I am the absence
> of field.
> This is
> always the case.
> Wherever I am
> I am what is missing.
>
> When I walk
> I part the air
> and always
> the air moves in
> to fill the spaces
> where my body's been.
>
> We all have reasons
> for moving.

>   I move
>   to keep things whole.
>   ("Keeping Things Whole")

This factoring of self and the world is manifestly a strategic with-drawal: it signals a consolidation of power rather than any sort of abdication. The *I* is now a catalyst for all the I is not.

Already in his first book, Strand began to employ the narrative or quasi-narrative formulas and the doubles that appear in so much of his subsequent work. I quote in full:

>   A man has been standing
>   in front of my house
>   for days. I peek at him
>   from the living room
>   window and at night,
>   unable to sleep,
>   I shine my flashlight
>   down on the lawn.
>   He is always there.
>
>   After a while
>   I open the front door
>   just a crack and order
>   him out of my yard.
>   He narrows his eyes
>   and moans. I slam
>   the door and dash back
>   to the kitchen, then up
>   to the bedroom, then down.
>
>   I weep like a schoolgirl
>   and make obscene gestures
>   through the window. I
>   write large suicide notes
>   and place them so he
>   can read them easily.
>   I destroy the living
>   room furniture to prove
>   I own nothing of value.
>
>   When he seems unmoved
>   I decide to dig a tunnel
>   to a neighboring yard.

I seal the basement off
from the upstairs with
a brick wall. I dig hard
and in no time the tunnel
is done. Leaving my pick
and shovel below,

I come out in front of a house
and stand there too tired to
move or even speak, hoping
someone will help me.
I feel I'm being watched
and sometimes I hear
a man's voice,
but nothing is done
and I have been waiting for days.

("The Tunnel")

End-rhyme, much muted, now hints at subterranean affinities. With the advertised suicide threat, Strand takes a shot at the confessional poets, whose methods he has always shunned, even inverted, but whose spectacle he has carefully studied. The use of obscenity as enticement requires no comment. The use of flight as a lure is as old as romance: Ariosto's Angelica and Spenser's Florimell had only to flee across the plain to engage all the knights for miles around in pursuit. Suspended flight may be more potent yet: it's the erotic lesson of a Grecian Urn, the perpetuation of desire by deferral.

Absence is power, and change, by a similar sleight, may clinch a static hold. "The Man in the Mirror," a slightly later poem, plays absence in numerous keys. The poem is too long to quote in any substance, but its broadest moves are the departure and qualified reappearance of Narcissus in the glass. Both moves, the disappearance and the return, aggravate the bondage of the lover, because the image restored is manifestly decomposing, forecasting yet another and final departure:

You stood before me,
dreamlike and obscene,
your face lost
under layers of heavy skin,

> your body sunk in a green
> and wrinkled sea of clothing.

Mortality makes even reflection faithless. The face loves death more than it loves its former self. It is change, quite crudely, that enters the mirror and narrows the lovers' alliance to some parody of the immutable.

> It will always be this way.
> I stand here scared
> that you will disappear,
> scared that you will stay.

End-rhyme, we note, continues to serve. Here it seals the stanza with a stroke like fate. Dreams of the double may always harbor a death wish of sorts, but they also harbor its opposite, the infatuating possibility of extending one's influence infinitely. Wherever I am, I am what is missing. I am, as Strand and Justice both have put it in separate poems, a horizon. The poet continues to mediate everything he has relinquished.

2.

Strand's quasi-narratives suggest narrative sources: Borges, Kafka, and the parabolic or paradoxical structures they canonize. Strand's formats are based on many of the same commonplaces these other writers employ: the symbiosis of complementary characters, the transposition of matter and context, of dreamer and dreamed, of writer and written. His later verse fictions embrace with increasing frequency the postures and devices familiar from Samuel Beckett: narrative or dramatic interminability, the story that insists on its own telling and invents the one who tells it, durability of voice amidst the longing for extinction, "the pain of revival and the bliss of decline." These phrases "From a Litany" appear in *Darker,* Strand's third book. In *The Story of Our Lives,* the echoes are more sustained:

> You want to wave but cannot raise your hand.
> You sit in a chair. You turn to the nightshade spreading
> a poisonous net around the house. You taste
> the honey of absence. It is the same wherever
> you are, the same if the voice rots before
> the body, or the body rots before the voice.
>
> ("In Celebration")

Strand borrows poetic shapeliness, then, from extrapoetic sources. He builds with three elementary figures: the circle that perpetuates motion; the Escher-like pattern that reverses foreground and background; and the asymptotic convergence of a line and a curve, Zeno's paradox maintaining decline and waylaying closure. The figures inevitably overlap.

The importance of Strand's narrative and dramatic models is structural, not thematic. This merits some insistence. When his critics use strategic affinities to account for affect and motive, when they intone not only *Borges, Kafka, Beckett,* but also *anguish, despair*—and they do—analogy has gone awry. It's not the sheer presence of wit that marks a different project, although the tenor and pervasiveness of Strand's wit provides a valuable antidote to solemn exegesis. But Borges and Beckett are witty too, and Kafka is some oracular equivalent; Beckett's more witty the closer he gets to the grave. No. It's Strand's pacing, his relative lassitude, that's the giveaway. The pallor behind Strand's narrative, the phlegm behind his very wit, betray an occupation distinct from those of Beckett and Borges especially. Though he uses the formal vocabulary of a metaphysician, Strand's subject is not the problem of perception. Not Berkeley's subject. Not Descartes's. Neither the anguish of consciousness nor its rewards. His methods are those of a sensualist; his subject, the disposition and deployment of power: erotica, politics, and especially the erotics and politics of passivity. Ultimate power resides with one who is only acted upon, who only provokes. The poems are poems of seduction:

> A train runs over me.
> I feel sorry
> for the engineer
> who crouches down
> and whispers in my ear
> that he is innocent.

He wipes my forehead,
blows the ashes
from my lips.
My blood steams
in the evening air,
clouding his glasses.

He whispers in my ear
the details of his life—
he has a wife
and child he loves,
he's always been
an engineer.

And after an effort at separation:

He rushes
from the house,
lifts the wreckage
of my body in his arms
and brings me back.
I lie in bed.

He puts his head
down next to mine
and tells me
that I'll be all right.
A pale light
shines in his eyes.

("The Accident")

Luminous morbidity has had no comparable heyday since Elizabeth Siddal first graced the pre-Raphaelite canvases. This is the exquisite transparence of Millais's Ophelia, languid unto death.

Certain versions of the accidental are chronically banished from Strand's poems: the accidental increments of material and social life, the detritus of fashion and wage labor and domestic arrangement, the shape of a chin, the lumps in the couch. But the syntax of accident chronically appears. Another way of putting this is to say that Strand suppresses the subjects of accident, the people and things that accident produces and leaves in its wake, in order to highlight the predicates of accident, the process itself. It is the shape of experience, not its contents, that interests him. In the system of his poems, events are wholly contingent or wholly fated, rather than caused or desired on a human scale. What happens happens for no reason or for the one reason (God, necessity, abstract pattern, the poet's whim), rather than for the intermediate reasons, the individual notations of human purpose. This is why the poems can be as shapely as they are, uncluttered by the merely anecdotal. In "The Accident," the speaker's imperturbability gives us our first clue that the anecdotal versions of cause and effect have been suspended, that the casual has supplanted the purposive. Even seduction works *through* the speaker, rather than at his explicit command. "The Accident" unearths the *casual* in *casualty,* the *causal* in both. Calamity provokes desire, enfeeblement arouses, contingency displaces will. Causality becomes diffuse or atmospheric. Compare these lines from "The Ghost Ship":

> Through the crowded street
> It floats,
>
> Its vague
> Tonnage like wind.
> . . . .
> Slowly,
> Now by an ox,
>
> Now by a windmill,
> It moves.

Because both ox and windmill are potential sources of momentum, the sentence is almost drawn to "it is moved" instead of "it moves." But the poem does not require the passive voice to preserve the ship's passive locomotion. The power to move is the power of contagion. Thus we say that a thought or a lover can infect the will.

In "The Kite," the longed-for catatonia exerts an influence equally pervasive:

> It rises over the lake, the farms,
> The edge of the woods,
> And like a body without arms
> Or legs it swings
> Blind and blackening in the moonless air.

With no limbs to work its will, the kite proceeds by insinuation, blind and blackening. The three long stanzas of this poem are haunted by recurring elements: lake, farms, woods, rain, curtain, wings, wind. In each stanza, their relative pressures are differently disposed. Causality passes through altered configurations. The elusive notion of origin goes underground, like Hamlet's ghost.

In the first stanza, the kite appears to have some hold on the weather. As it rises,

> The wren, the vireo, the thrush
> Make way. The rush
> And flutter of wings
> Fall through the dark
> Like a mild rain.
> . . . .
> An almost invisible
> Curtain of rain seems to come nearer.
> The muffled crack and drum
> Of distant thunder
> Blunders against our ears.

Of the line that runs from the kite to the weather, we know only that aural links and analogies predominate. The rain is never quite rain: it's a figure for sound, it's an immanent presence announced by sound.

In stanza 2, the kite string is held by a man who seems to precipitate whole seasons: "The wind cries in his lapels. Leaves fall / As he moves by them." In the final stanza, the elements of landscape resolve into the features of a parlor. Outside the rain fell like a curtain, and here "Inside the room / The curtains fall like rain." The poem is a hothouse where images bloom and cross-fertilize. The remnants of end-rhyme now intimate some hidden course of generation:

> Darkness covers the flower-papered walls,
> The furniture and floors,
> Like a mild stain.
> The mirrors are emptied, the doors
> Quietly closed. The man, asleep
> In the heavy arms of a chair,

> Does not see us
> Out in the freezing air
> Of the dream he is having.

The kite rises, still a conductor, and the man begins to wake. The kite may equal the dream or not; it certainly mediates the dream's authority. And, because parataxis is the mother tongue of dreams, equivalence and consequence are free to dissolve and reformulate. The panels of this poem are angled for resonance, not for reflection. Strand's is not a lapidary art. He relies not on taut juxtaposition but on the bland parataxis that loosens the will at its hinges. His methods mature with a chronic humor, their own slight fever.

As the poet moves further away from his earliest poems, the tension between line break and phrasing softens, enjambment nearly disappears. The simplest of syntactical patterns simply repeat; the eddies and stills of imagery even out. The poems encounter less and less resistance as they move down the page, until their progress becomes as frictionless as that of a kite or a ghost ship:

> We are reading the story of our lives
> which takes place in a room.
> The room looks out on a street.
> There is no one there,
> no sound of anything.
>
> ("The Story of Our Lives")

"The Story of Our Lives" and "The Untelling," centerpieces of Strand's fourth major collection, pursue the formal discoveries made in "The Kite." Each poem contains a story that contains a poem that steadily dismantles containment. As "The Story of Our Lives" proceeds, a man and a woman, side by side, consult the course of love in a book. Though love unfolds and doubles back, no point of origin or terminus appears, no point, that is, beyond which the mind might firmly declare itself to be outside the story:

> The book never discusses the causes of love.
> It claims confusion is a necessary good.
> It never explains. It only reveals.

In this way the book preserves the reasons for moving:

> It describes your dependence on desire,
> how the momentary disclosures
> of purpose make you afraid.

Books have promulgated desire before. When Paolo and Francesca, side by side, read the story of Lancelot and Guinevere, adulterous love renewed its kingdom: "A Gallehault was the book and he who wrote it; that day we read no farther in it" (*Inferno* V, 137–38). Gallehault served as a go-between for Lancelot and Guinevere. Boccaccio subtitled *The Decameron* "Prince Gallehault" and dedicated his book to *otiose donne,* idle ladies. The pattern for seduction is perfectly explicit, and perfectly vicarious. Strand's own poems mediate a vast inherited culture by appearing to build in a clearing. Their faithlessness is part of their pedigree, as faithlessness is the cement of love. Paolo and Francesca owed their fealty and their desire to Gianciotto, Lancelot and Guinevere to Arthur. The man and the woman on the couch must interpolate a breach of faith in order to perfect desire:

> I lean back and watch you read
> about the man across the street.
> . . . .
> You fell in love with him
> because you knew that he would never visit you,
> would never know you were waiting.
> Night after night you would say
> that he was like me.

Idle ladies are most apt to wander, so go-betweens play upon idleness. This explains why Strand's erotics should pass through languor to boredom at times. The man and the woman repeatedly fall asleep. The reader, left to stare at plainer and plainer walls, allows her thoughts to wander to Dante, Boccaccio, Borges, as the woman's thoughts wander to the man across the street. In his reader, Strand sows the seeds of the faithlessness that completes his hold. Mediation expands its inventory at every opportunity. Like a Greek messenger, the mailman in an early poem assumes the onus for news he bears:

He falls to his knees.
"Forgive me! Forgive me!" he pleads.

I ask him inside.
He wipes his eyes.
His dark blue suit
is like an inkstain
on my crimson couch.

' ("The Mailman")

In "The Story of Our Lives," "the rugs become darker each time / our shadows pass over them." In calamity and in burlesque, in even its modest moments, the book's ambition is limitless: to own what passes through it, to be the portal the past must enter on its way to the future.

They sat beside each other on the couch.
They were the copies, the tired phantoms
of something they had been before.
The attitudes they took were jaded.
They stared into the book
and were horrified by their innocence,
their reluctance to give up.
They sat beside each other on the couch.
They were determined to accept the truth.
Whatever it was they would accept it.
The book would have to be written
and would have to be read.
They are the book and they are
nothing else.

The book engineers its own supersession.

3.

In "The Untelling," the story of the past is handed from a third-person frame to a first-person frame and back again, four full cycles in all. Each narrator figures as a character in the story his counterpart tells. The two are alternate versions of one another, separated in time, and each produces the other, as the child is father to the man. The points of view draw nearer in time and place as the poem proceeds: a man writes a poem in a room overlooking a lake; the child in the poem himself observes a scene from the opposite side of the lake: each revision begins somewhat earlier in the story, somewhat closer to the house, and finally in the room itself. The setting is vaguely Chekhovian, bucolic, elegiac; there's even the sound of a breaking string:

> He would never catch up
> with his past. His life
> was slowing down.
> It was going.
> He could feel it,
> could hear it in his speech.
> It sounded like nothing,
> yet he would pass it on.
> And his children would live in it
> and they would pass it on,
> and it would always sound
> like hope dying, like space opening,
> like a lawn, or a lake,
> or an afternoon.

The period in which the past occurs presumably approximates that of the poet's childhood, but the women wear dresses whose hems are made wet by the dew. Hemlines haven't touched the ground as a matter of course since a family longed to stop time in a cherry orchard:

> *I waited under the trees in front of the house,*
> *thinking of nothing, watching the sunlight wash*
> *over the roof. I heard nothing, felt*
> *nothing, even when she appeared in a long*
> *yellow dress, pointed white shoes, her hair*
> *drawn back in a tight bun; even when*
> *she took my hand and led me along the row*
> *of tall trees toward the lake where the rest had gathered.*
> . . . .
> *It seemed as if the wind drew the dark*
> *from the trees onto the grass. The adults stood*
> *together. They would never leave that shore.*
> *I watched the one in the yellow dress whose name*
> *I had begun to forget and who waited with*

the others and who stared at where I was
but could not see me. Already the full moon
had risen and dropped its white ashes on the lake.
And the woman and the others slowly began
to take off their clothes, and the mild rushes of wind
rinsed their skin, their pale bodies shone
briefly among the shadows until they lay
on the damp grass. And the children had all gone.
And that was all. And even then I felt
nothing. I knew that I would never see
the woman in the yellow dress again,
and that the scene by the lake would not be repeated,
and that that summer would be a place too distant
for me to find myself in again.

The woman's dress takes its color from the sunlight the revenant watches before she appears, or gives the sunlight its place in his mind because she is about to appear. She guides him to the lake like a mother and leaves him like first love; he summons her to the place he holds for both. And, even as he knew that he would never see her in yellow again, he sees her so in memory and in this poem. The forfeits of will and the footholds of longing are deeply equivocal:

> His pursuit was a form of evasion:
> the more he tried to uncover
> the more there was to conceal
> the less he understood.
> If he kept it up,
> he would lose everything.

According to the paradox of aging and generation, everything must be given up if everything is to be gained; growing up is rather like getting into heaven in that regard. That regard only, presumably. The adult blossoms on the corpse of the child he was. The child he makes, in imagination or in the flesh, his consolation for mortality, is also the agent of usurpation. The poet is like the rest of humankind in this regard: he furthers his will not chiefly by testimony but by testament, by divestment. And thus the final lines of this poem:

He sat and began to write:
THE UNTELLING
To the Woman in the Yellow Dress

The dedication bequeaths the story to another, places it squarely in the hands of one who cannot help but appear, and in her yellow dress at that. She as she was, she as she was to him. As wills go, this one is quite a coup. In the courtship the poem enacts, the woman has played the role throughout of mediating third, the go-between for man and child. As long as man and child had to share the burden of narration, each could approach the other only by surrendering his own reality. The woman in the yellow dress is the agent in whom their stories overlap. By taking the story over, a matter she cannot refuse since her page is white, her part in the story is silence, she allows them to coexist at last in harmony, to assume their place in the fixed constellations.

4.

The strategics of will and testament reveal absence in its other aspect, as a hedge against mortality. Poem after poem in Strand's corpus makes this clear: when absence cracks, mortality gets a foothold. This is the other side of "The Man in the Mirror." This is why, "When the Vacation Is Over for Good," we find we are dying. This is why "The Guardian" is invoked as he is: "Preserve my absence. I am alive." Divestment and renunciation are forms of preemptive suicide:

I empty myself of the names of others. I empty my pockets.
I empty my shoes and leave them beside the road.
At night I turn back the clocks;
I open the family album and look at myself as a boy.

What good does it do? The hours have done their job.
I say my own name. I say goodbye.
The words follow each other downwind.
I love my wife but send her away.

My parents rise out of their thrones
into the milky rooms of clouds. How can I sing?
Time tells me what I am. I change and I am the same.
I empty myself of my life and my life remains.

("The Remains")

Strand plays with the formulas of masochism and self-immo-
lation, but the erotic and funerary aspects of divestment always
come down to this: a solemn striptease and a wonderfully irrev-
erent act of monument building. The concurrence of these oc-
cupations incidentally clarifies the equivocal status of discards
and the vicarious role of a readership. "I give up my tongue," says
Strand on the page. "I have omitted to mention my wife or
daughter." And by such ruses, he doesn't, he hasn't. Everything
named is preserved. Everything abandoned to language is there
to be taken up in another life, like the mummified food and
playthings in a pharaoh's tomb. The reader is consigned to
prurience. She watches the self enticing the self to love; she over-
hears; she oversees; and by such moves is taken on as permanent
overseer, the custodian in whose care the monument resides.

The Monument itself absents itself from the *Selected Poems.* Its
prose, however, is always and explicitly the prose of a poet, who
comes to its pages empty-handed. As "The Untelling" was dedi-
cated to the woman in the yellow dress, this volume is dedicated
with sublime humor and manifest coerciveness "*To the Translator
of* The Monument *in the future.*" The honor conferred does not
come free. (Strand has dedicated other poems to his most illus-
trious critics and to the illustrious editor through whom his fin-
ished poems pass first. The board of executors.) Again and
again the supposed translator is reduced to the most abject de-
pendence, his every insubordination second-guessed, his very
speeches of protest written for him. "I live in you," The Monu-
ment says.

Epigraphs play a prominent role in the book. Passages from
Thomas Browne, Unamuno, Nietzsche, Wordsworth, Borges,
and Suetonius, to name but a few, are yoked into a single dis-
course. (We should write, says Petrarch, as the bees make sweet-
ness, turning the various flowers into a single honey.) The poet
claims the inherited past as his to bequeath and, by the way, re-
hearses the origins of epitaphic verse in wayside interments and

epitaphs. *Siste viator,* The Monument reads. Stay, traveler. In Coleridge's epitaph, the interjection is "Stop, Christian passerby!"; on the seat in Wordsworth's yew-tree, "Nay, traveller! rest." As a legal will lays its hand on the living, as the Ancient Mariner waylays the wedding guest, The Monument stops the course of all who would continue outside its control. The Monument knows nothing indifferent; it knows only itself and its residue:

> Give us a blank wall that we might see ourselves more truly and more strange. Now give us the paper, the daily paper on which to write. Now give us the day, this day. Take it away. The space that is left is The Monument.
>
> (Sec. 45)

The Monument's "other voices" are more of the same:

> Sometimes when I wander in these woods whose prince I am, I hear a voice and I know that I am not alone.
>
> (Sec. 30)

The passage above appears in tandem with an epigraph derived from Saint Mark: the poet is not above an aggrandizing pun on his own name. The Monument's final words, appropriately enough, were not its own until it commandeered them:

> *To pass on, (O living! always living!) and leave the corpses behind.*
>
> (Walt Whitman, now The Monument)

What The Monument leaves behind is matter for a changing poetic—sanction too, if a cover illustration may be so read. Assuredly, the picture of mortuary architecture that adorned *The Late Hour* (1978) when it first appeared cast something of a shadow: the hour was late as death approached. On the other hand, this particular monument was put farther behind with each new page one turned. On the back of the book, the poet, still very much alive, regards his readers. Between covers, the writing follows the course of one who has decided to return from the brink of the grave, to leave death to its own devices. A poem whose absence I regret when I read the *Selected Poems* is "No Particular Day," in which the turning is first announced:

> Items of no
> particular day
> swarm down—
>
> moves of the mind
> . . . .
> that take us
> somewhere near
> and leave us
>
> combing the air
> for signs
> of change,
>
> signs the sky
> will break
> and shower down
>
> upon us
> particular
> ideas of light.

Sotto voce, the poet invokes what heretofore he has loudly banished. He has favored the generic for the authority it confers, furnishing his kingdom with everything in general and nothing in particular; but here he prepares to turn again to the accidents and givens that particularize experience.

In *Selected Poems* the lyric "Exiles" becomes the fulcrum for change, the site on which the work of restoration commences. Its first section follows the plot more or less of Albee's *A Delicate Balance:* a certain "they" find life disappearing around them and run to "us" to be taken in. In the second section, in what might be a prologue to the poet's later work, they reverse their course:

> And on their way back
> they heard the footsteps
> and felt the warmth
> of the clothes they thought
> had been lifted from them.
> They ran by the boats at anchor,
> hulking in the bay,

> by the train waiting
> under the melting frost of stars.

This reunion with the world does not exactly end in a wash of optimism:

> They lay in their beds
> and the shadows of the giant trees
> brushed darkly against the walls.

It is, nonetheless, a reunion of moment, and here are the gifts that accrue: St. Margaret's Bay, the North West Arm, Mosher Island, Wedge Island, Hackett's Cove, Fox Point, Boutelier's wharf, Albert Hubley's shack, a furniture store, a black baby Austin, brants and Canada geese, a mother, a father, an uncle, a grandmother, and Winslow Homer's *Gulf Stream*. The change is enormous, this change that begins with the final third of *The Late Hour*, and it's not imparted by proper names alone. If the ravelings and auras of personal memory find quarter for once, this is not to suggest that the earlier poems had no sources in biography, or that the current poems never invent or lie. The *appearance* of personal history is what was not encouraged before and is very much encouraged now.

When place names appear, as they occasionally do, in the earlier poems, they are poised on the scales of dislocation. As "The Last Bus" moves past Lota's park in Rio de Janeiro,

> The ghosts of bathers rise
>
> slowly out of the surf and turn
> high in the spray.

The image is designed to capture the material imagination but cannot be solved in material terms. Far from being comfortably "placed" by setting, the reader encounters deliberate disorientation. So with distinguishing items of clothing or social class. "Let us save the babies," an early persona proposes,

> You shall wear mink
> and your hair shall be done.
> I shall wear tails.

To underscore a retreat to animal instinct, Strand has borrowed his perspective from the hoi polloi, who refer to certain fancy male attire as "monkey suits." Since "The Babies" is a Vietnam-era parable about the survival of the fittest generation, the playfulness is apt, but is hardly a genre painter's approach to circumstantial detail. So with memory. In his earliest poems, the memory Strand was interested in was the memory he could engineer, the memory he could become. In poems written since the late 1970s, he grants some affection to the merely historical, some credence to the merely found, and he diversifies the methods of provoking recognition. No attentive reader will expect biography to "solve" a good poem, or will underestimate Strand's loyalty to the methods and discoveries of fiction. But when the poet begins to grant the past and the reader some license of their own, this loyalty is being reconstrued.

The final sections of *Selected Poems* include work as purely lyrical as any Strand has written; the phrases are more extended, the mimetic strategies far less guarded, than any the poet has used before. One poem, based on an ominous survey of the Thames in *Bleak House,* assembles a central sentence of twenty-eight lines, whose eddyings and sweep reproduce the course of the river itself. As to the elevation of the quotidian, one final example demands our attention. The poem has provoked a fair amount of skepticism, even among Strand's admirers, and may therefore be a useful test of his continuing strength and perspective. The poem is named for the thing itself: "Pot Roast."

> I gaze upon the roast,
> that is sliced and laid out
> on my plate
> and over it
> I spoon the juices
> of carrot and onion.
> And for once I do not regret
> the passage of time.
>
> I sit by a window
> that looks
> on the soot-stained brick of buildings
> and do not care that I see
> no living thing—not a bird,

not a branch in bloom,
not a soul moving
in the rooms
behind the dark panes.
These days when there is little
to love or to praise
one could do worse
than yield
to the power of food.
So I bend

to inhale
the steam that rises
from my plate, and I think
of the first time
I tasted a roast
like this.
It was years ago
in Seabright, Nova Scotia;

my mother leaned
over my dish and filled it
and when I finished
filled it again.
I remember the gravy,
its odor of garlic and celery,
and sopping it up
with pieces of bread.

And now
I taste it again.
The meat of memory.
The meat of no change.
I raise my fork
and I eat.

The senses that feed on well-being here are those most resistant to the embrace of language. The taste of a roast, the smell of an onion have the power to translate the speaker to another time precisely because they resist translation. The sensations of taste and smell withstand the dilution and obfuscation that readier equivalents inflict upon the process of sight. The reader, however, may understandably choke a bit upon this particular version of the lime flower tea and madeleine. In the context of anecdote, the transporting powers of garlic and celery are credible, if uninspiring. In their figurative capacity, as revisionist versions of Proust, as the specific and composite key that unlocks the past, they cannot help being somewhat parodic: pot roast is about as close as a poet could get to generic food. Not mother's Christmas cardamon bread, not even Aunt Mabel's own barbeque sauce. Even a sympathetic reader might think at first that Strand has miscalculated tone: the language—"juice of carrot and onion"—gets awfully reverential at times; the poet might almost be eating the host.

And, indeed, this disproportion is meant as a clue. Strand's closing lines are modeled on the closing lines of a Herbert poem, a poem about the final communion in heaven:

> You must sit down, sayes Love, and taste my meat:
> So I did sit and eat.
>
> ("Love III")

The meat is the meat of transubstantiation. Even without the detective work, we know something of this from the rhythms with which Strand's poem draws to a close: those rhythms argue that "meat of memory" and "meat of no change" are in earnest. The earnestness reads like a callow mistake, until we find that the second helping is literally a double take. The past has been used up, as has the vision that Herbert believed in, as has the cultural nexus that fostered a sensibility like Proust's. And then the change: as when the bread is bread no more, the empty plate is filled again, and everything lost restored. The mother's shade enacts her blessing, and the agnostic has his sacrament too, the meat of memory to be savored like hope. And what of the humor?—the past recaptured in a pot roast, Jesus on a fork? Strand has accommodated radical disjunction before, purest burlesque and sobriety in a single poem, but never did disjunction entail a greater risk. What this poem has in mind, and brings to mind, precludes the somnambular voice that Strand so often used in the past to solve the problem of tone in a hybrid production. The title—"Pot Roast"—partakes of that poker-faced hilarity that alerted us to double meaning in earlier poems, but it's not reinforced by obvious gestures in kind. The poem relies on internal transformation and accomplishes what it does by ensuring that it will first be underestimated, even dismissed. In this manner the poem mimes its subject and confesses to a diminished version of the myth it reenacts. History repeats, with some chagrin. Tempering solemnity with parody and sentiment with plainsong, the poet makes his stubborn case for celebration.

5.

Having channeled his most distinctive accomplishments into a poet's prose that sidesteps or cagily reroutes generic expectations, Strand is now experimenting with various reconstructions of the lyric voice. He has relaxed his censorship of quotidian detail; he's trying a gentler hand with the past and a lusher version of literary homage; he's practicing a less austere, more personalized and impure fable. Are the poems a dilution of the former enterprise? The poet himself has signaled a shifting of loyalties: "I'm really less interested in writing magazine verse or individual poems than in creating a literary spectacle . . . a little like *Barthes on Barthes*" (*Missouri Review* [summer 1981]). But Strand has always enacted the spectacle he describes. If all writing distributes allegiance between an audience and a subject of regard, if all writing occupies a place on the continuum that runs from the presentational to the contemplative or exegetical, Strand's characteristic work has steadfastly been of the former kind. The poems were rhetorical, which is to say they were designed to have effects upon an audience; the self was a rhetorical construct built in view of that audience; the argument was all ad hominem. Their beauty notwithstanding, the poems written since *The Monument* may prove to be something of a sideline. On the other hand, as a poem like "Pot Roast" should alert us, the play of presence and absence continues in all its vitality, even when, on first glance, presence seems to have become less problematic. The new bifurcation of voice, one part spoken by an altered lyric, one part by all that is left of the old, may signal the start of a dialogue we will all do well to attend to: the flower *and* the bee.

A Cradle of String

"The soul in paraphrase" was Herbert's happy paraphrase for the devotional discipline he called *prayer* and the poetry we call *metaphysical*. May Swenson has called her latest book *In Other Words,* thus reinscribing the poetry of paraphrase and conspicuously gesturing toward that prior book whose words are the originals of humanity's. Bacon called that prior book the book of nature. May Swenson might be prepared to call it that as well. Certainly, the better half of her poems devotedly inventories the sensuous and sensible aspect of things. And this work is dense with a double materiality: that of language—heavily paratactic, maximally alliterative—and that of the observable world. In her descriptive mode, the poet's insistent treatment of sounds as things—her heaping up of syntactical and metrical abutments, of echoing vocables, of appositional metaphors—seems quite palpably to be an act of invocation:

> Part otter, part snake, part bird the bird Anhinga,
> jalousie wings, draped open, dry. When slack-
> hinged, the wind flips them shut. Her cry,
> a slatted clatter, inflates her chin-
> pouch; it's like a fish's swim-
> bladder. Anhinga's body, otter-
> furry, floats, under water-
> mosses, neck a snake with white-
> rimmed blue round roving eyes.

("Waterbird")

The soul in paraphrase is the soul at risk, the soul out on a limb. And in the final section of *In Other Words,* the poet takes to the branches of a banyan tree for a thirty-three-page allegorical

---

First published in *Poetry* 154, no. 4 (July 1989): 233–38.

sojourn. The tree the poem is named for sends out a parasitic sprawl of root and branch: the poem propagates analogously, by means of sprawling high- and low-cultural spoofs. Its narrator, who assumes the contours of a woolly monkey for the duration of the fable, takes as her consort a white cockatoo, whom she acquires by jailbreak from a cage in the municipal library in Coconut Grove, Florida. These heroines, Tonto and Blondi, make a mixed marriage of the sort that used to unfold in comic strips when wives were always buxom, or on prime time when a masked white man was sure to command loyalty among the nobler specimens of a primitive race. The mission of the poem, however, is neither domestic subversion nor freelance outback justice but a sequestered meditation on the "purpose of life." The cockatoo, fresh from its library, provides an endless stock of literary tags: the fable makes glancing allusion to famous plots from that of *Paradise Lost* to that of "The Murders in the Rue Morgue." In a climactic mirror vision, the cockatoo and the monkey are revealed to be two of the Ages of Woman, the one (the bird) an old-fashioned, new-minted child of two, the other (the primate) a figure of brutal decrepitude:

> Her stomach poked out and sagged, partly hiding her slumped, hairless pudenda, and her flattened breasts hung, the left longer than the right. . . . Arms and lower legs were thin, but the flaccid thighs, the buttocks and the coil of fat at the waist hung in jellylike bags.

The poem's mild-mannered deployment of cultural cliché and cultural satire only feebly prepares us for this harsh nay-saying to vanity's wish for transcendence. And, as coda to the crueler vision, Halley's comet appears, the span between its anticlimactic returns just the length of a human being's decline into age. Clipped-winged, the cockatoo returns to its cage and succumbs to genre, intoning its new tag phrase oracularly: "The purpose of life is / To find the purpose of life." This collapse into tautology is meant to resonate with the achieved tenor of spiritual quest: the chastened spirit recording its dilemma in a partial breakdown of language. But the breakdown of language here is something more mundane than a crisis of faith would account for, and the poem's ironic strategies do not quite solve the tonal problems of prolonged self-dramatization.

A similar entanglement with truism afflicts "Some Quad-rangles," which was the Harvard Phi Beta Kappa poem for 1982. Occasional verse is not much honored in our time, nor prac-ticed with deftness by more than a handful. The genre was al-ways a thorny one, and we tend now to be embarrassed by the conventions that maintain it and by the patronage system of which it is the coin. In the poem she read at the Harvard com-mencement of 1982, Swenson records the late-twentieth-century sprawl of university students on the green commons and uphol-stered library chairs of their campuses, records this sprawl from the bemused perspective of another, more formal generation, one that suited different protocols and different manners to the privilege of sponsored study and reflection. Deriving a moral from the ebb and flow of protocols, the poet commis-sioned by the Harvard and Radcliffe chapters of Phi Beta Kappa, at length and in blank verse, exhorts her audience of graduating patrons to shun conformity. Swenson gains some small torque by smuggling the very form and substance of a high school valedictorian speech into the venerable halls of ivy, but as to conformity, her poem is rather a cautionary than an exemplary instance.

Despite her title, and despite her devotion to banyan, cocka-too, saguaro, and egret, Swenson does not submit her "other words" as a form of deference to some prior order. Taking the world of nature and the world of words for her twin playgrounds, she flaunts poetic conceit and poetic prerogative. A thing is so because she's taken a fancy to saying it's so. The waterbird's tail may be "a shut fan dangled," a family of egrets may be "Three White Vases," snow may be "an ermine floor," and saguaro may be shamelessly anthropomorphized ("Flowers come out of their ears"). Metaphor in these poems is a celebratory exercise in in-genious ornament, immoderate, unreclaimed. In their sprightly disregard for decorum, these ornaments resemble the meta-physical conceit, but, unlike the metaphysical conceit, they ex-hibit no strenuousness and no catalytic capacity. Swenson has no interest in the labor that makes of metaphor an argument or metamorphosis. Hers are frictionless conceits for the most part, the mind's eye eyeing its own pleasure; poetic figure delightfully embellishes but does not alter or explicate the underlying object of regard. There are exceptions, of course, as in "Eclipse Morning," where the sequence of mixed and overdetermined metaphors both mimics and manifests the difficulty of accommodating solar eclipse to the scale of earthly comprehension, or in "A Day like Rousseau's Dream," where the female genitalia, "a pod of white unpainted canvas," are at once the center of revery and the space that eludes it. For the most part, Swenson's poetic project finds its fable in "A Thank-You Letter," where the gift consists of its wrapping—a "cradle of string" and its durable transformations—not in any posited "inside." Stanza after pleasurable stanza, Swenson's poems find shapeliness in self-reference and pure assertion: well-wrought vases made from a glimpse of egrets.

There are dangers in this imperturbable refusal to measure the figural imagination by its service to argument. When image fails in its magic, the language quite simply misfires. While "Shift of Scene at Grandstand" doggedly pursues its inert equation of seasonal change and theatrical scene shift, more delicately nuanced observation is overwhelmed. Though "Shuttles" does eventually marshal a fairly lively indictment of the phallic imperialism embodied in the American space program, it first bogs down in a great deal of ill-regulated jargon: "All systems are Go" and so forth. In "Strawberrying," a late-season excursion to the berry fields is glossed with the language of violence and predation (the picker's hands are "murder red"; gray berries are "'families smothered as at Pompeii'"), but the metaphoric subplot, for all its hyperbole, remains inconsequent.

In "Blood Test," the figurative imposition is disturbing for quite different reasons. I quote the poem in full:

Alien, the male, and black. Big like a bear.
Wearing whitest clothes, of ironed cotton scalded clean.

I sat in a chair. He placed my arm on a narrow
tray-table bound in towel. As if to gut a fish.

"Mine the tiniest veins in the world," I warned.
He didn't care. "Let's see what we have," he said.

Tourniquet tied, he tapped his finger-ends inside
my elbow, smartly slapped until the thready vein fattened.

Didn't hurt. He was expert. Black chamois wrist and hand,
short square-cut nails, their halfmoons dusky onyx.

I made a fist. He slid the needle, eye-end in, first try,
then jumped the royal color into the tube.

Silence. We heard each other breathe. Big paw
took a tuft of cotton, pressed where the needle withdrew.

"That's it!" Broad teeth flashed. Eyes under bushy
mansard hair admired, I thought, that I hadn't flinched.

I got up. Done so quick, and with one wounding. I'd as soon
have stayed. To be a baby, a bearcub maybe, in his arms.

Swenson records a scene of strictly contextualized intimacy between two persons of different sex, race, and professional expertise, his on display in the phlebotomy lab, hers in the poem that renders it. Amidst this quiet negotiation of curiosity and power and vulnerability, the "Big paw" and the "black chamois wrist" are not trespasses in any simple sense, but neither are they retrieved from trespass by the expressed desire to be a bearcub "in his arms." Immersed in the transcription of her home-spun phenomenology, the poet, like her kindred, the tourist and the colonialist and the ethnographer, casts a proprietary eye on the spectacle of cultivated estrangement. And, though the implications of its own methodology are actively ignored in this poem, poetic conceit is by nature an appropriative move. In this instance, the subject with whom metaphoric liberty is taken is neither a cactus nor a waterbird but a member of the race whose own liberties have been, repeatedly and to our shame, conspicuously abridged; this subject, moreover, belongs to a professional class (he is a medical technician) whose authority is all too easily overridden by the retrospective authority of the poet. The clichés of estrangement, including the ameliorative fantasy of desire with which the poem closes, have an extrapoetical history and an extrapoetical politics of which this poem pretends to be innocent. But look what innocence produces: the artificial and unconvincing sequestration of politicized subject and poetic method allow cliché to hold uncontested sway. And between the races, between the classes, between the sexes, as history has taught us, cliché is a dangerous thing. Innocence will not always serve. I am sorry to say it.

Where Swenson's methods are transformative, and delightfully so, is in the territory she modestly refers to as "comics." In a Halloween poem, Swenson renders the season's propitiatory masking by pursuing a child's game of switched consonants: "The roldengod and the soneyhuckle, / the sack eyed blusan and the wistle theed" work their sweet mischief in "A Nosty Fright," where the "nasty fright" we summon for pleasure's sake lurks very obligingly behind the "frosty night." And when has the ghost of Gertrude Stein been more happily heard from? In "Giraffe," which the poet calls "A Novel," she sets language before us in all its emphatic thingness: "Giraffe is the first word in this chapter. Is is the second word," and so forth. The project that appears so frontal soon becomes sly: "Is is the second word is the second sentence in the first chapter," for instance. That sentence appears at first to be a misprint for its equally accurate but more facile second cousin ("Is is the second word in the second sentence in the first chapter"), but it is we, not the typesetters, who have faltered. The more fully the poem turns its back on the world of conventional signifying, the more fully it claims to be a world unto itself. As long as the layers of self-reflection and reification are backward looking, the poem called a novel still safely endorses our expectations of referentiality. But with "Chapter 7" ("This is the first word in this chapter and the third and seventy-fifth word in the tenth chapter") the reification becomes anticipatory. Summarizing the past and the future in a single arc, the poem completes its divorce from the world of referents and wraps itself in imperturbable closure.

The rigors here, as must be clear, are of the sort that animate a ledger sheet: the playfulness is not calculated to inspire affection. "Giraffe" works in territory that has been very cumbersomely theorized of late: it works with the simplest of tools and with immutable composure. And its virtuosity lies in this, that the poem's "other words" are the only ones sufficient to its cause. What is the measure of truth in these sentences? Self-reference alone, except for that supernumerary, the giraffe— the useless one, the beautiful, the one with nothing to graze upon, the one with the lofty view.

3

Eight Women Poets

Sharon Olds, *The Dead and the Living*

The pleasures of this book—those it takes in the world and those we take in the poems—are frankly erotic. The imagery is voluptuous and near-at-hand, the voice direct and richly modulated, the conceits—of mountain climbing in "Ecstasy" or grade school math in "The One Girl at the Boys' Party"—are limpid and readily assimilable. The background narrative, as in Olds's first book, belongs to family romance and sexual coming of age. The body is her credo and her inexhaustible source of metaphor. None of its dramas—puberty, aging, childbirth, hunger, mutilation, miscarriage, sleep, arousal—is beyond her clear-eyed powers of transcription: even a child lost in the fourth week of pregnancy can find a body in these poems, can float for its wrenching moment as "dark, scalloped shapes" "in the pale / green swaying water of the toilet." Olds is an eloquent celebrant—I know no contemporary her equal here—of sexual love and its extrapolation in a mother's erotic ties to her children. She also, perhaps inadvertently, records the radical invasiveness of erotic proprietorship: Olds takes in these poems an owner's liberties with her son's erections and her daughter's immanent pubescence. Such causes and such a gift for celebration are enviable, and are meant to be: much of this poet's work might be described as a poem in her previous volume was titled—"The Language of the Brag." Displaying a connoisseur's way with the sensuous image, an unabashed advocacy of the flesh, and a seemingly uncensored penetration of domestic life and its progressive revision of female consciousness, these poems

---

First published in *Poetry* 145, no. 1 (October 1984): 36–49.

can afford to be free with their clarity, as a beautiful woman can afford to be free with photographers.

In the first of five sections in *The Dead and the Living*—the "Public" half of "Poems for the Dead"—immediacy and passion afford insufficient guidance, despite the white heat of the poet's protest over a murdered Rhodesian mother and child: "Just don't tell me about the issues . . . I've got eyes, man." Few readers would wish to tamper with the general lines of partisanship in these anti-elegies, espousing as they do the victims of famine, of war, of political torture (in Iran, in China, in Chile), of racial hatred, and of sexual exploitation ("The Death of Marilyn Monroe"), but our ready-made consensus is somehow part of the problem. These poems anthologize approved causes; their repeated origin in photographs merely enhances the discomfiting impression of scrapbook pages. If their purpose can be neither to proselytize (we already agree) nor to inquire (they explicitly disavow "the issues"), their primary work, by design or by default, is to set the stakes for the book they introduce, to make an implicit claim for the stature of subject matter and the moral authority to come. And, as if to betray such a self-serving project, the poet/persona later compares her cruel father to Nixon resigning from office in shame and to the murderous Shah of Iran; she portrays her bullying older sister for a full poem's length as Hitler invading Paris. The "public" poems wish to cast off all issues but those of human suffering and its deep counterargument, the stubborn faith and sublime intelligence of the human body, its survival and its eloquent reproduction (in children, in photographs, and in imagination). But the opportunistic deployment of public figures in "private" poems reminds us that passionate advocacy cannot suspend "the issues" indefinitely. When poetry taps and exploits the charged realms of human extremity and public opinion without taking on the real burden of history and choice, it willy-nilly evolves a politics of its own, and one that can only be called exploitative. Olds's portraits of individual anguish in Chile or in racially splintered Tulsa gain much of their momentum, after all, from the increments of public opinion they claim to transcend.

We badly need an intelligent political poetry in America. In *The Dead and the Living*, I find the most convincing political formulations in poems to the living family, where Olds is willing to anatomize the workings of power and principle and partisanship before our eyes. "Coming home from the women-only bar" in one poem, she confronts the contrary claims of her beloved, sleeping son: "Into any new world we enter," she writes, "let us / take this man." The moment is a small one as world government goes. The competition between gender loyalty and family loyalty and strategies for the mutual liberation of the sexes constitute less momentous dilemmas, no doubt, than genocide and mass starvation, but they are worthy issues, nevertheless, and they are the issues more deeply interrogated in this book.

Mary Oliver, *American Primitive*

Mary Oliver is surely one of the purest lyricists we have. She is our Herrick, she works in song. But she is also a conundrum, for contrary to Herrick and contrary to our contemporary masters of lyric formalism—our Merrills, our Wilburs, our Hollanders—Oliver appears to be almost wholly uninterested in the strategies of artifice. She is not much moved by the works of humankind, and she somehow contrives to love the world more than she loves language, no common feat for an artisan who works in words. For Oliver, the significant world is primarily the world of nature—of the pond, the bramble, the damselfly, the humpback whale. She will extract the lessons of mortality from the last blaze of autumn or the leap of a bobcat or the hardy reappearance of skunk cabbage in early spring, but she does not savor landscape and fauna chiefly as pretexts for metaphor or meditation. She does not unveil ecology or treks through the woods as self-portrait writ large, and she specifically eschews the fashionable plunder of environment for the sake of poetic ornament—the overstuffed catalogues of clotted detail that smother or preclude the real work of curiosity. Hers are spare, lean poems of celebration, Sapphic in their lineaments and in their distillation of appetite, keenly disciplined to luminous transcription of the visible, touchable, edible world. Mary Oliver almost seems to have taken pastoral, that most artificial of all literary conventions, at its word, to have hied herself off to the springs and the hills and found there the sources of poetry.

All her seeming transparence, of course, is not for a moment the helpless by-product of rustic ingenuousness, despite the *primitive* of this book's title. If Oliver finds her primary subjects outside the apparatus of literary and high-cultural heritage, her method is primitive only in the sense that it is originary, determined, and able to derive first principles before our eyes. If there is a drawback to lyric of this sort—the lyric as plainsong, the lyric as a devout and steadfast rhetorical posture toward both subject matter and the listener—it is that the voice, unaccompanied and unbound by traditional schemes or by syncopations of syntax and poetic line, must carry the burden of continual freshness. The short line Oliver favors—predominantly one of two or three feet—serves not so much to govern phrasing and musical stress as to control the pacing of apprehension and to establish a necessary margin of silence, so that the poems may be built in a clearing; the white space mimics that repose which enables the self to look outside itself with intensity. The constant reinvention of the musical phrase within the confines of such resolute plain style is a daunting project: Oliver's syntax is liable to go drab when it is not taut. Her lineation and her vision can go stale together, as in these flagging repetitions:

> they're there—quick
> as beetles, blind
> as bats, shy
> as hares
>
> ("Moles")

> they traveled
> like a matched team
> like a dance
> like a love affair.
>
> ("The Snakes")

Elsewhere, the continuing postures of wonder will exhibit signs of strain: an overabundance of directive punctuation—exclamation points and colons in particular—or an overly resonant slowing of pace. But it is a measure of this remarkable volume that the very mention of lapses feels a little curmudgeonly and more than a little ungrateful in the face of poems like "Mushrooms," "The Lost Children," "Fall Song," "Something," "Honey at the Table," "Happiness," and "In Blackwater Woods." They give us the courage for "joy / before death"; they take us by the hand "from one bright vision to another."

Celia Gilbert, *Bonfire*

Celia Gilbert's greatest strengths are those of an imagist, and her very best poems ("The Still Lifes of Giorgio Morandi," "The Stone Maiden") are governed by single exquisite conceits. An admirable second rank ("The Gardener," "Spells," "Return," with its magnificent final lines) is grounded in the candors and the clear-eyed sympathies of a generous heart. But the sensibility is a fragile one and liable to a thousand dilutions: to literal-mindedness ("'The Empire of the Senses,'" "Lot's Wife"), to mild melodrama ("Storm Watch," "Nature," "The Cow"), to sentimental elevations of diction ("the words we dare not express," "Have you envied me for giving birth?"), to regressions of voice (which do *not* reproduce a childlike perspective; see "Clyde"), to cliché ("I must travel back to the woman / I was"). The long final poem in this volume ("Lot's Wife") juxtaposes the destruction of Sodom and Gomorrah to the bombings of Hiroshima and Nagasaki. Insofar as Gilbert casts a skeptical eye on the shared, dismaying status of the chosen servants of the God of Wrath, this juxtaposition is a mobile and a suggestive one. But when the poet mines her stories for an ethical hierarchy, with men on the low end (bigots, sycophants, bomber pilots, patriarchs) and women on top (life-givers, truth-tellers, comforters, victims), she succumbs to a self-congratulatory ideology. In this last regard "Lot's Wife" is not an isolated instance.

Gjertrud Schnackenberg, *Portraits and Elegies*

Gjertrud Schnackenberg's limpid versions of prosodic formalism remind us that meter and rhyme are the mnemonics of the universe, a litany of clues to its secret accords and echoes and, by the way, a wonderful alibi for directed rumination. For those gifted with curiosity, the labor of fulfilling a contract with form can be the enabling distraction that conditions remembrance and uncovers the structures of understanding. Sometimes memory can be a deceiver: seeking to resolve a poem about pursuing her dead father in a dream, Schnackenberg inadvertently transcribes the final lines of Stanley Kunitz's "Father and Son." But the same sweet solemnity and the same easy conference with inherited forms can also summon up the deeper layers of cultural memory and can lend to a new insight the contours of familiarity—these are the prosodist's real powers and ones with which Schnackenberg is liberally endowed.

Portraits and Elegies does not house the usual miscellany of a first collection; it is as little congenial to randomness of structure as to that of musical form. The book is a triptych: two sequences—one of elegies to the poet's father, one chronicling the many generations of a house in South Hadley, Massachusetts—are divided by an extended portrait of "Darwin in 1881." Elegy and portraiture do not distinguish the separate groupings of poems in the book but are rather the reciprocal aspects of its single, retrospective posture. The first sequence, "Laughing with One Eye," interlineates remembrances of the poet's father with moments from the proximate aftermath of his death. "19 Hadley Street" traces a reverse chronology back to the early eighteenth century, with discrete returns to the narrator's present tense: so an old man's final illness, for example, precedes his auspicious moment as a bridegroom; a comfortable Sunday dinner between-the-wars gives way to an antebellum debate on the subject of abolition. Darwin's portrait, cast in the year before his death, is erected upon an extended analogy to Prospero's abdication in *The Tempest.* The recollective methods of the book lend considerable poignancy to its individual passages of human happiness and security, of course, but the poems are not backward-looking in the usual sense: they also contrive a robust framework for comprehension and celebration, what the poet at one point calls "a metaphysics of impersonal praise." The dead father was, after all, an historian, and this volume is pervaded by his credos as well as his personal presence.

Within her carefully plotted sequences, Schnackenberg's breadth of sympathy accommodates some welcome variations of form and tone. In "The Meeting in the Kitchen, 1740," for example, her habitual pentameter contracts to a four-foot line that mimics the hypnotic chanting of a witch's spell. Here and elsewhere, the poet expends some gentle wit on the credulities of departed eras. When nineteenth-century townsfolk, in the sway of an itinerant preacher of doomsday, hear a young prankster blow his tin horn from the roof of 19 Hadley Street, one Esmerrianna Knott

> then calmly bent to close
> Her hem up with a gathering thread
> So sinners left on earth could not
> Look up her dress as she arose.

Between "The End of the World, 1843" and the samplings of eighteenth-century witchcraft, the poet balances a present-day survival of the other-worldly. In "Halloween," a precocious young masquerader disavows the general superstition, but the narrator demurs with a difference:

> the King of the Dead

> Has taken off his mask tonight, and twirled
> His cape and vanished, and we are his
> Who know beyond all doubt how real he is:
> Out of his bag of sweets he plucks the world.

In such a fashion, the sequencing of poems contrives to set the permutations of belief and experience in dialogue with one another.

In a book of so much sophistication and delicacy, I am hard put to account for the pervasive impression of ingenuousness. Some part of this may be attributed to the unusually frontal quality of so much full rhyme, uncluttered syntax, and repetitive meter (the poet is sometimes rather mesmerized by her iambs), but the effect is also a reflection of the poet's particular exegetical posture. Schnackenberg occasionally posits some recalcitrance on the part of nature or the past ("Beyond our touch," "Our isolated little world of light"), but the world she in fact portrays is one of remarkable legibility, a world of undertows and overtones, to be sure, but none of them seriously intransigent, none hostile to interpretation. Before the felicitous conflation of her musical habit and her habits of mind, the world quite magically unlocks itself. In "The Living Room," the present inhabitants of 19 Hadley Street have hung a picture of the enthroned Madonna near the piano, and, as the narrator practices Bach, the Virgin is distracted from her Book of Hours:

she finds it rich and right,
Such music out of black dots on the page,
Symbols, the world a symbol from her height,
Great voices rising like smoke from time's wreckage.

As while the composer labored on his Fantasies,

His wife awoke the first on earth to hear
These silver lines beginning, plucked, revolved,
Unearthly trills spiraling up the stair,
The night dispelled, Leipzig itself dissolved,
And Paradise a figuring of air.

It is the poet, in her faith and skill, who twines the two perspectives into a kind of love knot—the mutual invention of heaven and earth.

Susan Tichy, *The Hands in Exile*

This book draws primarily upon a period in 1977 when the author lived on a kibbutz in northern Israel, so it finds its paths among the tutelary figures of the M-16 and the tractor and the cow. Its pages are filled with the homiletics of armed hostility and manual labor; its surfaces have been polished to a fine laconic finish. Having no mind to be mistaken for "the German city-girl," Tichy liberally dispenses her four-letter words and her tough-minded vignettes, rendering the tastes and the smells and the narcosis of work, the subtle cross-hatchings of physical danger and racial suspicion and importunate collective memory; her setting also lends her a vocabulary for the dynamics of sexual impasse and sexual imperialism. Tichy has learned, quite possibly from Yehuda Amichai, how much momentum and modulated irony is to be gained by meeting the burden and the borrowed resonance of history with an unclouded rhetorical simplicity. Like Amichai's, her chief economies are those of compressed anecdote, of parable and proverb, of witty, self-dramatizing direct address, and of supple understatement. Here are the final stanzas from "The rich don't have children . . .":

"No rape at all?" said a French correspondent,
shaking his head. "What kind of army is that?"

"I'm sorry," said the Arab girl, "but it is true."

"I'm sorry," said the paratrooper
who gave me a lift to Bethlehem.
"We can't do everything. We are so few."

And here are the first lines from "Shabbat Moming":

> God, I am sorry.
> The veterinarian from Haifa
> will be here in the morning.
> The cows must come down
> from the Golan Heights today.

Tichy's major advantage, for evenhandedness and perspective, is also her major limit in this book: she has come to Israel as a visitor to gather material and experience; she can leave. She does not, however, lift the problems of vicariousness and borrowed danger to explicit consideration, as Carolyn Forché has so shrewdly done in *The Country between Us*. As if to underscore the unresolved dilemma, the second section of *The Hands in Exile* reads like something of an anticlimax. Without the grounding polarities of the author's stay in Israel, these miscellaneous poems linger like a pallid postscript until "The Soul in the Valley of Kidron" reanimates the exile.

Erica Funkhouser, *Natural Affinities*

If focus and proportion, attentive good nature, and respect for one's craft are signs of modesty, then Erica Funkhouser's is a modest enterprise. She is blessedly unwilling to write the endless poem that stars the self and raids the world for stage props. From "Paper Clips":

> they are not trombones to open my mouth;
> they are not glass tubes
> to conduct my experiment

Funkhouser finds her best occasions in the quotidian—in a pipe wrench, in a hand saw, in a heap of starfish, in a child's first four-letter word—and she lets us watch while she primes the pump—a series on "Tools," a series on animals, a series to the beloved, a series to family. If the format sounds rather like an exercise book, and the accomplishments, yes, a little lackluster, and the lapses, yes, betray some tendency toward tepidity and preciosity, the author nevertheless has genuine gifts: an affinity for the just image, a reliable composure, an unforced pleasure in the transforming power of words.

Mekeel McBride, *The Going Under of the Evening Land*

These poems privilege the unfettered imagination, the surface play of fancy and invention, the signposts of sensibility. At their best, McBride's negotiations between expectation and creative license achieve an exquisite balance. The following is a full stanza from "The Green Gazebo":

> And they are still sitting in the gazebo.
> Grass at the bottom of the wooden stairs
> is so wet with dew one might believe
> that earlier in the afternoon, a woman
> in a yellow dress sat there,
> stringing necklaces. And, distracted,
> spilled a glittering vial of glass beads
> that now catch and magnify
> street-lamp light, shining
> with the slight patina of displacement.

The first line, with its architectural whimsy and the unbracketed duration of present progressive, establishes a congenial setting for the gestures of romantic caprice. The next sentence appears to be aimed at evocative description but introduces a similitude (the woman in the yellow dress) that reads more like a non sequitur. When the poem's internal branching leads to necklaces, we appear to have lost our path altogether. Only after a coy full-stop is the woman reclaimed for analogical plausibility by means of a connecting image (the spilled glass beads, which bring us back to dew). Our momentary indirection and the woman's free-floating suspension in a plot of her own (stringing the as-yet-un-explicated necklaces) resolve themselves in such a way as to augment the interdependent pleasures of digression and linearity; we've been sweetly toyed with. The final modifier ("shining / with the slight patina of displacement") deftly summarizes not only the immediate sensory subject (the lamplit beads) but also the rhetorical transactions from which we have just emerged.

Regrettably, McBride too often contents herself with lesser amusements. The poems are filled to bursting with the frills and fritillary of creative writing, with taffetas and water-marked satins, with tears and roses and endless silks. The poet has a weakness for random hyperbole ("paints with terrible precision," "sleepless and weeping / with awe"), for atmospheric circumlocution ("filled with whatever the moon / has left behind," "the plain black and white / of what is always here"), and for downright preciosity (two butterflies "congratulate the sky / with a fragile disbelief in sorrow"). She pays homage in more than one instance to the work of Charles Simic, but, where Simic will cannily manipulate thumbnail narrative and aura against the backdrop of folktale or parable or bleak postwar neorealism, McBride will too often exercise her liberties in a vacuum. Without the foil of generic expectation, the most extravagant imagery ("the silver Tiffany serving dish / of the moon," "azure butterflies drowning / beautifully in the finger bowls") is flaccid; the materials of fancy remain inert. When McBride contrives for herself some tension between pretext and improvisation (the mere alternation of nostalgia and burlesque, or of wit and reserve, is not a substitute), she writes with great authority (see, for instance, "The Form and Theory of Ordinary Joy" and "On the Nature of Autobiography or an Admission of Concern"). Without such tension, the poems too easily lapse into confectionery.

Rita Dove, *The Yellow House on the Corner* and *Museum*

On the cover of Rita Dove's first book, *The Yellow House on the Corner*, the author regards us full front and full bleed (the borders of her portrait flush with the borders of her book) from a monochromatic photograph (in yellow, of course) taken by her German husband, the novelist Fred Viebahn. On the cover of

Museum, the implicit self-portrait has undergone a striking series of translations: we are confronted by the black-and-white photograph, cropped and ornately framed, of a painting by the German artist Christian Schad. The painting is a double portrait of two sideshow entertainers, a white man naked to the waist, with grotesquely overgrown lower ribs and scapulas, and a black woman seated below him, a woman accustomed to dance, we are told in a subsequent poem, with snakes. The painting and the poem share a name in which the author has found her own: "Agosta the Winged Man and Rasha the Black Dove."

In the nomenclature of those who police the boundaries of affiliation, a "yellow" Negro is one accused of sellout, a black man or woman who has been compromised by too much currency in a white world. In the breadth of her subject matter and her self-presentation, Dove peripherally summons up the specter of such nomenclature, but, rather than submitting to its hostile categories, she redeploys them to accommodate the multiple strains of her voice and understanding. To be sure, the central sequence of American slave narratives in *The Yellow House on the Corner* sits a little uneasily between two sections of embellished autobiography, poems about growing up among the artifacts and trappings of the American middle class. But within the slavery sequence, dramatic monologue and compressed narrative exhibit considerable discipline in the uses of cross-cultural imagination: the poems have an ear for the decorums of eighteenth- and nineteenth-century written prose ("Belinda's Petition," "David Walker [1785–1830]"), an eye for the power of books among those who cannot read, a voice for individuals caught in the crosshairs of competing cultural loyalties and for community dismembered along the fault lines of relative privilege and deprivation (a house slave considers her sister in the field, a Negro driver helps in the capture of runaway slaves). Surrounding this sequence, Dove's stylized treatments of adolescence and personal history seem much less clear in their ironies and decorative gestures—I'm not always certain which are meant to be undermining. But there are other poems in *The Yellow House* that travel in space and setting as the slave poems travel in time, poems that capture vignettes of postwar Germany or a trek to the Sahara, poems that weave subtle parables of provinciality and distrust and entrapment on the one hand, of xenophilia and migration and vicariousness on the other ("Small Town," "The Bird Frau," "'Teach Us to Number Our Days,'" "Ö," "The Son"). I like to think of these as a second sequence, albeit a scattered one, set in dialogue with the black history sequence—a kind of thinking tourist's meditation on internal exile. In "Ö," the poet instructs us in her one word of Swedish: "Shape the lips to an *o,* say *a.* / That's island." Dove demonstrates what it is to speak one language through another and shows how much of solitude this entails; she shows us also that a double tongue can mean a double point of view and therefore a kind of stereoptic vision—an incomparable strategy for depth perception.

In *Museum,* as its title and its cover artwork announce, the author has advanced to full prominence these preoccupations with displacement and multiple frames for point of view, frames that are superimposed rather than synthesized. The book is structured and conceived with great deliberation and coherence, from its section titles and sequencing to its epigraphs, its attributions and its dedication: "for nobody," reads a page at the front, "who made us possible." The book's recurrent thematics are those of light and shade, the exotic and the domestic, reticence (with its furthest limit a nearly Delphic impenetrability, like the hush in a museum) and disclosure (whose extreme, in the sideshow and in the painting by Christian Schad, circles back to meet its opposite). On both geographical and temporal coordinates, the sweep of the book is large: from Argos to Erpenberg to the poet's native Ohio, from the Western Han Dynasty to the nuclear age. Nor are these distances a species of lush window dressing: Dove believes in history and is capable of mining it for the lucid intersections of imagination and pragmatic ways-and-means, for the junctures where solitary virtuosity finds both its intractable limits (as Catherine of Alexandria was "deprived of learning and / the chance to travel") and its most urgent motives. And according to that other perspective on history, as captured in books or museums, Dove is concerned to render the altered status of a subject when it has been set aside for special delectation, like the fish in the archaeologist's stone or like Fiammetta in Boccaccio's mind: the creature lifted to visibility by the pressure of a gaze is also partly stranded there, unsponsored even while it is wholly possessed. In technical terms—their use of the luminous image, their economics of plotting and musical phrase, their reliable modulations of syntax and levels of diction—these poems continue the same expert craftsmanship that marked Dove's earlier work. In their collective argument—and it is a profound one—they go much farther.

The reconstruction of a cultural or a familial past has become a very shopworn enterprise in American poetry: Polish Americans, Norwegian Americans, Jewish Americans, Chinese Americans, the hundred-and-one varieties have practiced their domestic and ethnic archaeology as a passport to poetic voice and personal exoticism. Cyrus Cassells (*The Mud Actor*, 1982) did much to derail the habitual pieties when he placed his reveries of the American South and familial history ("When an English exiled Jew / married an African princess / all hell broke loose") on a par with two extravagant "previous incarnations"—in fin de siècle France and in war-savaged Hiroshima. In *Museum,* Rita Dove brings her considerable intelligence and equilibrium to a similar project, debunking the smokescreen of naive cultural wistfulness (which casts us as plants, with "roots" and a passive knack for growth and a native capacity for light) in order to investigate the true architecture of our longing. This is the larger argument of self-presentation in *Museum,* where autobiography and the broader history of blacks in America appear less prominently as explicit subject matter than as angles of vision and as hermeneutic keys. (Read "In the Bullrush," for example, and think what Moses knew of exile. Even the cane, removed from water, finds water again in the rock.) Dove knows the difference between nostalgia and history, she knows the marketability of prodigious ornament and unnatural alliance (the tortured wings in the torso of a man, the habit of dancing with snakes), she knows the exchange rate between pleasure and danger, and she knows the place of strangeness in our unbroken labor on the fiction called "home." The status of "guest worker" is a broader one than euphemism would have us believe: no faction among us but is here on sufferance and liable to expulsion. Here is Dove's "Primer for the Nuclear Age":

> At the edge of the mariner's
> map is written: "Beyond
> this point lie Monsters."

Someone left the light on
      in the pantry—there's
      a skull in there on the shelf

that talks. Blue eyes
      in the air, blue as
      an idiot's. Any fear, any

memory will do; and if you've
      got a heart at all, someday
      it will kill you.

4

My Lady's Damask Cheek

Despite disclaimers ("you can't talk about the weather / it's like saying my lady's damask cheek"), the poems in James Schuyler's *Selected* are weather altogether: the inner weather of urban pastoral and out-of-the-closet, in and out of the sanatorium, pill-popping, name-dropping, unobtrusively financed, neoconfessional ennui. Wage labor is as rare and camp and alarming a presence as are women in these pages; the story is deeply class inscribed ("men who don't make much aren't much / for spending what they do / on glass eyes, tooth-straightening devices . . . , nose jobs, dewenning operations / a country look prevails"). By contrast, Flora's fair-faced children (siblings to the damask rose) occupy a privileged position in Schuyler's poems as in his Manhattan apartment and in the recreative landscapes—New England, maritime Canada, Long Island, and upper New York State—defined by affluent Manhattan and its rituals of retreat. The fair-fleshed human is rendered with abandon and often with abandon's double edge, as is the physiology of sex. If not the weather then that other atmospheric locution—nature's reiterated round of days and seasons—is lushly documented in these pages and unabashedly made a figure for the soul and its longings. These conflations of desire and Nature belong to a tradition of which Romanticism was the mere by-blow. Witness Narcissus, whose self-regard at last took the form of a flower.

The features described above—parodic, traditional, self-incriminating, self-absorbed—are the deliberate features of a poetic project that has achieved considerable public acclaim by flaunting itself as coterie. The paradox is an old one. Main-line Petrarchists have always pretended to write for private circulation

First published in *Poetry* 155, no. 5 (February 1990): 351–60.

while making public spectacle of the heart's most inward throbbings. Schuyler writes his poems in an epistolary mode, the mode that affects indifference to publication; he names his correspondents, flatters and reproaches them, inscribes them as an exclusionary community of taste. When he crosses the epistolary mode with that of the exhibitionist daybook (menus, shopping lists, the reiterative record of bowel movements, insomnias, erections, ingestions of antidepressants and Antabuse), Schuyler crosses the lineage of Sidney and Ralegh with that of *Clarissa*. The love lyric plays midwife to the novel in these poems; they derive their heat, their sometimes considerable length, and their excruciating detail from the logorrhea of forestalled seduction. Schuyler's is a poetry of sentiment, even of sentimentality, and of passive-aggressive ironies. It is a poetry, at times, of ravishing beauty and a poetry, always, of enormous structural intelligence. It is a poetry whose deployments of genre and rhetorical address make it a central document in the interlineated history of style, politics, and sexuality.

What is the nature of this rhetorical address? Schuyler's announced coterie takes its contours from the worlds of art, New York, and homosexuality. His short list of classic erotica runs the gamut from *The Faerie Queene* and *Hesperides* to *The Gay Insider* and *Run Little Leather Boy*. His work makes stylistic discriminations (high camp, East Fifties Queen) that will be obscure to portions of the general public. Some contrasts in decorum may be useful here. In the work of Elizabeth Bishop and William Meredith, the distinction between the common reader and the intimate, or front-line, reader is chiefly encoded in dedications and in the ungendered second-person. In Merrill, most notably in his Ouija *Commedia,* the domestic partner and the circle of admired companions are made the agents of aesthetic and prophetic mediation, while the unremitting urbanity and high-cultural affiliation of poetic voice serve to educate a readership into sensibility, to fashion, as Spenser does, an audience of courtiers. In Ashbery, the elusive second-person serves to obscure rather than to precipitate distinctions between the initiated and the great unwashed. Party to a dispersed, metaphysical dialogic, Ashbery's *you* is a fluid property, modulating to refract the reader, the self, the rhetorical subject. Schuyler's *you* is easier to locate in the phone book, is bound by circumstantial evidence, is even called upon to *supply* circumstantial evidence:

> What I can't remember is the name of my New York
> doctor: "Murray." But Murray what? I must have it
> Written down someplace, and if I haven't "you" can tell me.
> When you read this poem you will have to decide
> Which of the "yous" are "you."
>
> ("Morning of the Poem")

Without missing a beat or crossing a line-break, the *you* thus taunted with contigency or indeterminacy reassumes the familiar outlines of the poem's dedicatee, the painter Darragh Park:

> you will have to decide
> Which of the "yous" are "you." I think you will have no trouble,
> as you rise from your chair and take up your
> Brush again and scrub in some green, that particular green,
> whose name I can't remember.

Thus between amnesia and amnesia the poet coyly drops and retrieves again the drapery of dense quotidian, the gossipy tissue of "fact" that makes a field or figure of the self. Just glimpsed between the double erasure and the double exposure, Schuyler's problematized *you* fleetingly acknowledges a layered and a shifting audience, as much the product of wavering fidelities and attention spans as of the tensions between the inner circle of friends, lovers, and cognoscenti and the outer circle of duller, straighter, differently anxious and aroused lookers-on, that circle reduced to buying the book. Even for those on the mailing list, the letter when it arrives "may not say what you hoped / Or distraction robs it of what it once would have meant" ("Hymn to Life").

Schuyler relies, in short, on overlay and overkill, on abutment and conspicuous indecorum to prompt the uneven comprehension and unsteady collaboration of a readership on whom he in turn bestows a mixed regard. Not for him the homogenizations of consensus Culture. He flaunts the world's flattest line ("This pear tastes good") and drops the torch passed on by his masters ("the waves come yapping / something about 'wine dark'"; "A / Quote from Aeschylus: I forget"). Rendering landscape, he aggravates the timeworn coercions of anthropomorphism by drawing his metaphors from the marketing end of human manufacture ("The trees / say *Wesson*. *Mazola* / replies a frog"; "In Y's and V's and W's / an elm ascends / smoothly as an Otis Elevator"). Time killed, time savored, the comforts of toast and jam, little revenges against "the friends who come to see you / and the friends who don't," mortality's debris: the midden-heap of consciousness takes its outline from a number of circumstantial correlatives. In "The Payne Whitney Poems," the poet derives truant rumination from the enforced tedium of the psychiatric ward; in "The Morning of the Poem," from a vaguer recuperative stay at his mother's house in upstate New York. In "The Crystal Lithium," syntactical and associational slippages render the reciprocal contamination of buffered senses, the flash and shutdown of chemical normalcy. But the distinctive contour of Schuyler's loquacity in each case exceeds its occasion; mimetic plausibility is not the chief interest of these poems. They are written to charm and to affront. Narcissism is their vaunted affliction and their offering. They come to tell us that the world is a world of vested interests and of difference. They are not always nice.

As to my lady's damask cheek, two aspects (apart from the fact that the lady's in drag, of which more later): mingled in it like the red and white are venerable traditions of sexual desire and lyric poetry. Schuyler's *Selected Poems* is filled with erotic tribute, tracing a fast and a fraught course through the history of love-in-verses. Among the poems from his first book, *Freely Espousing*, Schuyler includes a translation of the second of Dante's *Rime petrose*, a sestina in which form is explicated as the structure of obsessional desire, a structure later codified by Petrarch and thence by all the propagating sonneteers. Also from *Freely Espousing* and drawn from another branch of the same lyric tradition is Schuyler's elegy to the orgasm ("'The Elizabethans Called It Dying'"), a poem whose associational detours trace the para-ejaculatory drift of mind. In subsequent volumes the love poems come in droves, some (like "Eyes") pure loveliness and some ("Steaming Ties") limp sentiment and third-class puns. "A Head" is classic blazon, a poem whose sumptuous description discloses the proprietary haggling, the fragmentation, and the fetish implicit in this subgenre of lyric praise. It is also a back-handed play on words: the boy with the beautiful head appears to give head too. By heaping up brand names ("You . . . kicked / off Gucci loafers") and the other detritus of appetite ("The night is filled with indecisions / To take a downer or an upper / To take a walk / To lie / Down and relax"), Schuyler insists on the currents of banality and consumerism that modulate erotic address; desire, as he shrewdly narrates it, is the story of renewable discards. With deflationary self-exposures ("'Can't / you be content with / your wife and me?'"), Schuyler willfully destabilizes the tone while mirroring the structure of neo-Petrarchan complaint, and his negotiation with literary precedent is typified by backhanded homage to Donne's "The Relic," in which he rejects, along with fine phrasing, the sanitizing, idealizing, out-of-the-body Christianizing justification of heterosexual love: "This hair bracelet won't tell us much."

Women play the unenviable role of triangulations in these poems, bartering chits in the conduct of homoerotic affairs. Their transit is sometimes brief, as in the negligent traverse of simile ("Summer apples . . . a finger bruise on thin skin / brown and silently reproachful as your wife's black eye"), and sometimes more prolonged, as when Lena Horne is made the currency of pickup in "Pop Tunick's long-gone gay bar." Horne sings "Mad about the Boy" on the jukebox; the speaker keeps plugging his money in and making a play for one of his fellow patrons. Even in its "straight" version, the music is a thumbnail history of appropriation: sexual passion smolders a bit when sung by a black woman to a paying public that is largely white, heterosexual, and male. Smoldering heats up when the performance is restaged by a constituency (gay) with a history of oppression and a motive for subversion as significant as are the singer's own. The abrasion produced by such an appropriation is part of its capacity for titillation: Schuyler's social critique, if such it is, does not much hunger after the homogenizing prospect of cross-gendered or cross-cultural common cause. The frictive pleasures of the scene at the gay bar endure long past their original moment; successfully picked up, the poet's lover makes Lena Horne the sticking point in a drawn-out, teasing debate about sexual coding and predilection ("he / thought it was East Fifties queen / taste"). Even in verse, Lena Horne is a trope with a history: in Frank O'Hara's "Biotherm," passion makes its louche declaration between two tributes to Lena Horne: "'I am a woman in love,' he said."

A more convoluted figure of gendered triangulation provides the punch line in "Letter to a Friend: Who Is Nancy Daum?" In a love letter, the poet describes the French lamp on his desk-top—glass stemmed, glass shaded, and signed by the maker, "Daum, / Nancy." "Hence I surmise / she made / or, at least, / designed it. / Who *is* Nancy Daum?" Nancy Daum is, of course, a joke of double inscription, the naive correspondent's failure to distinguish between place name (Nancy) and first name (Nancy). She is woman as misprision or, worse, faux pas. But she is also a faux faux pas, the throw-away that binds the writer and his intimate correspondent in their superior command of cultural encodings. These cultural encodings include the exaggerated gender play of butch and femme. The signature of "Nancy Daum," described in a postscript, supplements the other coy signature beneath which it occurs: "(signed)— / all my / —you know— / *ton* / Dopey." It is thus another version of the "camp name" Schuyler elsewhere reveals as "Dorabella." The play at stake in the camp name is the play that determines who may be a player: "If anybody called / me by my camp name / nowadays I'd sock them."

Women, for the most part, are not among the players in this book. Oh, they will do for a supporting friendship or two—autobiography's spear carriers—but they more typically serve to mark the bounds, by being outside the bounds, of taste. They are irritants (the maid "stinking up the house with household ammonia," the "assistant" who makes breakfast and lunch ["I think I'll / let her take the laundry / out; she needs the exercise"]). They are the common coinage of malicious gossip (the "future Duchess of W.," who got where she's going by being "a circus in bed"). They are the self-exposing purveyors of phobia and false orthodoxy ("'I got her number: / "Why did you tell him homosexuality is a neurosis?"' / I said, 'She said / She didn't say it, but she did'"). The free expression of what we now call sexual preference, including the varieties of heterosexuality, have too often entailed hostility between and within the sexes, though there are those who wish to believe that this need not be the case. Hostilities are rife in Schuyler's poetry, no less so because they are conducted ironically, often within literal quotation marks. The contest, as he stages it, is about the mastery of nuance; who governs the subtlest transactions of taste can establish his taste as normative.

Erotics are commodity everywhere, but the pace and pressure of the marketplace are central to the libidinal self-portrait Schuyler draws. He cruises the supermarket ("trying to get a front view of / him and see how he was / Hung"). He ogles the delivery boy ("funny-faced, skinny and muscular, red-gold hair, and, sigh, / wears a broad plain wedding ring"). He vamps ("I wish I had a rose / Or butterfly tattoo . . . Here on / my arm or inner / Thigh, small, where / Only the happy few / Might see it"). He writes the unstoppable memoir of sexual debacle: shore leave liaison with a soldier who turns out to be "trade," the apartment ripped off by the drugged-out lover of a lover, the chase-scene-with-a-deadly-weapon staged around a kitchen table. And everywhere—past and present, fantasy and fact—the odds on flesh and passion are leveraged by age. Rueful, vindictive, and comic by turns, Schuyler writes the ill-sorted tale of Love and Time. In middle age, he is a lover perpetually "on the sniff," though mostly quiescent ("I haven't beat my meat in days") or impotent from Antabuse, a lover increasingly sidelined by the premium set on youth ("now men my age are not / Interested in me, they seek out beauties, blue-eyed, / blond and tanned . . . there's no democracy"). The vamp and the complaint are too stylishly deshabille to be the helpless revelations of feeling or circumstance; they are rather the knowing, portending postures of rhetoric. That is to say, the poet has designs on his readers, who are at once potential conquests and interloping lookers-on (both versions of "the happy few").

What is more, the poet has the means and the motive to expose the dynamics of readership: his postures are heuristic. Played out as soap opera, confessionalism's vamp and complaint are invitations to voyeurism; played out as laundry list, confessionalism's excessive documentation is voyeurism's surfeit and negation. Schuyler plays both sides of a transaction quite perilous to self-esteem. Schuyler is kiss-and-tell; he's a name-dropper and a snob; he's archivist of his own bon mots ("when our best poet was invited / To review one of your little offerings I said, / 'Won't it be like / Reviewing your reflection in an oil slick?'").

He is also a savage satirist of just such self-reflexive merchandising ("'Oh / I was beautiful, oh the most / Famous men all fell for me and slipped it up / my cooze'"). The past tense is the nastiest indictment of all.

Death is the subplot; death lurks behind every parenthesis. Dining with a friend at McFeely's, the bar at the old Terminal Hotel, the poet feeds on a menu of memento mori ("Dining Out with Doug and Frank"). McFeely's, Terminal: New York is riddled with puns as with memories, and every urban setting bears the weight of things that are no more: the mirror glass at Gage and Tollner's, the Hudson River ferries, the Singer Building, Fairy Soap, a lengthening list of friends and enemies ("At least twice when / someone I knew and hated / died . . . I smiled and laughed out / loud"). Though it happens behind the arras or happens offstage ("I wouldn't go / when he wanted to see me when / he was dying of leukemia"), death is the engine that makes the plot proceed: "Why is this poem / so long? And full of death? . . . 'Enough is as good / as a feast' and I'm a Herrick fan." The questions are rhetorical. Exemplary Herrick sat down to a feast (his Julia's breasts fresh cheese and cream, her nipples strawberries), but he smelled the stench of death between two cherry lips (and thus advised women to hide their rotten and rusty teeth). Exhorting virgins to seize the day, Herrick lodged beneath the language of compliment the steely reminder that appetite is mortal too. Why is Schuyler a Herrick fan? And why is his poem so long? Death is the mother of alibis. From death we want distraction.

Death is also the mother. In Schuyler's late long poem "A Few Days," he makes his most extravagant display of tedium and laundry lists. The poem is chockablock with the details of diet and interior dec, of pill consumption ("seven Sleepeze, two Nembutal, / the scoffed pills, three / antidepressant pills, a red pill that controls the side / effects of the antidepressants,") and cologne consumption ("Help! my Eau / de Portugal is half empty"), of personal hygiene, wardrobe, and insomnia—all the proliferant, excremental documentations of identity ("Here is my Blue Cross/Blue Shield number: 11223677 / H08"). Elusive as ever, identity is the ghost in the machine. Also in this poem, Schuyler makes his most extravagant display of maddening, manipulative dependence in matters practical: it is others who cook, who clean, who work for money, who care for the dying. Dying is what we're all up to ("A Few Days // are all we have"), but dying with a difference and for good in the course of this poem is the poet's mother. He wasn't there; he'll stay home from the funeral; the phone call with the news is what finally shuts his story down. The business of the story is diversionary: "don't dwell on the grave, which yawns for / one and all." Answering the voracious yawn with the yawn of induced and remedial boredom, Schuyler makes the good effort, the penman's effort, not to dwell on the grave but to live with it. A mock-up of Freudian parable, the poem is an elegy whose subject is everywhere apparent and everywhere repressed.

Selected Poems concludes with two lyric celebrations of the poet's newest crush and "secretary," a blond "Apollo" who comes four days a week to make breakfast. But Apollo loves E., another young man, whose mother is worried. "I'm / going to tell her how / lucky her son is," the jealous poet resolves. In an earlier poem, Schuyler describes gaining access to his first crush by playing courtier to the young man's mother, on whom the real plot was necessarily lost. What are these mothers to him? And why should he use them as leverage? It's been twenty years since Stonewall, but mothers still tend to worry. Mothers are living proof that the story of gay life must still be conversion narrative—or subversion narrative, the ironizing mastery of distance from one domestic generation to the next. Generation: the oppressive, tautological hegemony of procreation. Mothers are in their very bodies—the ones that made children, the ones that made us—the life that must be thrown over. In his newest ode to the "only and always beautiful," Schuyler identifies his Apollo by first name, middle name, last name, by lineage, and by hometown. We're back to blazon, the thwarted version of kiss-and-tell—just in case the young man's mother has yet to figure things out. Petty blackmail, the ingenious double play of petition and promotion (in a new variation on the old Petrarchan formula, the young man celebrated for his beauty launches his own career in poetry), publicity as enticement, publicity as revenge: all's fair. Sweet love plays hardball.

Schuyler came of age "back in the Turkish bath days"; he still puts "gay" in quotes sometimes. His ironies record the extent to which homosexuality in our culture has had to construct its discursive and presentational styles under seige. Its styles are among the most brilliant and alluring we have: capable of the most complex cultural work, the most sophisticated, speculative self-fashioning, the most finely shaded and radical wit. Schuyler's poems, with their apparent record of compromised intention and disarray, are in fact the agents and repositories of consummate stylistic glamour. It is no accident that his corpus of indecorum is also a corpus of impeccable technique—his lineation alone would furnish a manual of style. Despite its displays of vulnerability, and they are rife, despite its capacities for entertainment, and they are sublime, Schuyler's poetry is not meant to be ingratiating, nor is it best honored by deferential readings. The poet claims full privileges for ruthlessness and sentiment both. "I / am troubled by hatred for / the dead," he writes. And also, manifestly, for the living. There's no understanding the love in these poems—its plenitude, its fever, its omnivorousness, its recoil—without crediting the hatred.

5

Little Sun

In the twenty-seventh chapter of *Middlemarch*, George Eliot bequeaths us an elegant parable about point of view. "An eminent philosopher among my friends," she writes,

> who can dignify even your ugly furniture by lifting it into the serene light of science, has shown me this pregnant little fact. Your pier-glass or extensive surface of polished steel made to be rubbed by a housemaid, will be minutely scratched in all directions, but place now against it a lighted candle as a centre of illumination, and lo! the scratches will seem to arrange themselves in a fine series of concentric circles round that little sun.

That little sun is Pamela Alexander's conscious subject and the fulcrum of her lyric project. So, for example, Amelia Earhart's plane becomes "a tiny gear that turns the world," and a seafarer falls asleep to "the cabin's tilt and tilt / about the hammock's axis," gravity confirming for once the inherent self-flattery of private perspective. This self-flattery is sometimes the butt of Alexander's satire, as in a poem called "The Dog at the Center of the Universe," but in poem after poem this author rather celebrates than queries the transformative powers of the seeing eye. From the vantage point of Earhart's plane, "the Red Sea is blue; the White and Blue Niles, / green; the Amazon delta a party of currents, / brown and yellow, distinct." The flyer's singular perspective becomes a corrective to the muddying conventions of inherited nomenclature and collective imagination.

Or does it? Five lines later, the shining sea is "wine-dark," colored with a Homeric epithet that somewhat confounds "the

Review of Pamela Alexander's *Navigable Waterways*, first published in *The Boston Review* 10, no. 3 (July 1985): 28.

serene light of science." The pilot, the epithet reminds us, is a figure for the poet here, and point of view is a liberty as well as a discipline. The watery globe has two aspects: the one a field of vision ("the planet in its veil of weather"), and the other vision's instrument (the ocular globe). Homer's epithet in Greek means literally "wine-*eyed*," and the idiosyncratic view is clearly Alexander's favorite form of intoxication.

Though Amelia Earhart appears explicitly in only two of the poems in *Navigable Waterways,* she dominates the volume as a tutelary spirit for the poet's flights of imagination. On Earhart's last, unsuccessful flight over water, her plane "staggers with the weight of fuel, / becomes lighter and then / light." The sea on which the pilot practices her art of navigation is also the sea in which she drowns, but Alexander wants to find in "The Way Down" (the second Earhart poem) another version of "Flight" (the first). The poet argues for her heroine's apotheosis, for vision consummated rather than thwarted: "lighter and then / light."

In the white squares of the navigator's map and of her own stanzas ("consider . . . paragraphing as paper sculpture"), Alexander draws epic to scale. "Carelessness / offends the spirit of Ulysses," writes the adventuring Earhart, so Alexander's poetry is a poetry of fine distinctions. The book is mapped in four quadrants: after "Parts of a Globe," the poetry moves increasingly inward, to "Interiors" and then to "Natural Forces," which might justly be called "A Private Weather." Foreign adventure is progressively domesticated, brought into the drawing room with the English ivy, the "china," and the oolong tea. The sweep and textures of time become spatial, the freeze-frame and the end-stopped stanza are favored over the musical phrase, until the poem becomes a species of still-life, Ulysses housebound and bound in a book. With some notable exceptions, especially in the section governed by Earhart, Alexander's aesthetic is that of the fragment; her concept of the lyric is not words-with-music but words-with-music-in-mind, words shaped by a missing score. She calls her final section "Libretti."

The considerable virtues of this poetry are its disciplined economies, its wit, its self-possession, its playfulness, and its serious ambition to anatomize experience (Alexander suggests that we regard her parataxis as a species of cubism). The dangers of this poetry are primarily those of contrivance. The author will bring her poem to a halt for the sake of a pun, either grammatical ("Two parts. Often it does.") or orthographical ("IV. / Ivy that is"), and she loves a riddle to distraction. Homemade riddles can render the familiar strange, devising a kind of ingenuous phenomenology and a pleasant inductive labor for the reader, as when we try to guess *dry-dock* before the poem names it for us:

> I stand where the water will part.
> Only a diver or a dolphin
> will see the hull from here
> after the boat is launched.

Inherited riddles may unearth the secret accords in language and give some top-spin to rumination, as in these punning lines from "Vines": "A polygon has many angels. / How many cousins to the ounce? / How many weasels to the once?" A notorious cul-de-sac for theologians becomes a pleasure garden for the poet.

But there's a difference, finally, between word puzzles and metaphors, and one tires of moves like these: "I have rented a burrow for the winter; / if it were a donkey I would ride to see you," and "Here, a Q: // a british line." The burrow and the Q are virtual discards, once they've given the poet a chance for her sleight-of-hand; fine ground rules for a crossword but not for a figure of thought.

Navigable Waterways is populated by solitary, separable objects and perceptual acts—parts of a world in their nimbuses of absence. If the discrete gestures of mind and the material world aim to be component parts of a whole view, they are as often in these poems the disparate remains of failed connectedness. The danger of Alexander's rather willful dissection of language and experience is not that it leaves the emotional story out of the picture but that it gives the emotional story uncritical sway. "Your eyes look past me," the poet writes, "I want to be something to you." Given false license by the surface play of language, the cry of the heart is left to too-ready a paraphrase: "So the you I'm calling to, / the you that is me, / the one who wants to tell me / everything I know, / is both real and invented."

Alexander privileges solitude (Amelia Earhart crashed in the Pacific with a copilot, according to my sources, but the poet prefers her alone with her thoughts and her sinking plane), and the solitude of the imaginative microcosm is Alexander's chief poetic premise. If, on the page, her "fine series of concentric circles" are at times too thinly ornamental and, by a common correlative, somewhat too liable to sentiment, these problems of method have a genuine thematic ground, which may point this talented writer to new solutions in her subsequent work.

6

Literacies

Jane Shore, *The Minute Hand*

There are species of ornament that aspire to a place on top of the shawl draped on top of the piano. Jane Shore's poems are memorabilia: they cultivate the leisure and faceted pleasure of retrospection; they favor the miniature and the artifactual; they are tender toward kitsch. Their habitual manufacture is a kind of filiating description with which the poet embellishes some previously vested, inherited piece of human handiwork: a planter's clock, an Egyptian tomb, a set of nesting Russian dolls, a Persian miniature, a German barometer, a set of jackstraws, a home movie, the glass slipper that houses a wristwatch with Cinderella painted on its face. Like the fairy tale used to package the wristwatch, the imaginative configurations that animate these poems are hand-me-downs by design: the poet recycles the variegated vestments of collective imagination, that she may stitch her own affectionate connections with the past and with human community. This poet happens also to be a quilter of considerable accomplishment, and one is tempted to find in the latter activity a paradigm for her methods in the former.

Standing shoulder to shoulder in this book with the crafted toys of imagination are a group of family portraits: framed miniatures of the poet's shopkeeper father, the poet as a young girl, the poet in love. And, as in any such domestic gallery, the contours of narrative emerge: love's fraught negotiations in the family-of-origin (the father constrained and given form by earning a living, the girlish persona constrained and given form by the arrival of a usurping younger sibling) merge with love's fraught negotiations in the family-of-choice (the persona and

First published in *Poetry* 151, no. 5 (February 1988): 419–36.

her beloved and their several surrogates constrained and given form by the rigorous grammar of coupling). Cinderella and Thumbelina lend their stories to reworked parables of sibling rivalry and sibling aspiration. The graduated set of Russian dolls becomes a figure for the progressive reinvention and propagation of the self. The planter's clock yields up its kernel of mortality in the painted figure of a farmer's wife, who illustrates the seasons but is herself stranded in time, unable to harvest its fruits. Sometimes the moral unveiled in these poems is just what we feared it would be: in the wake of a lovers' quarrel, the protagonist watches boxers on TV and mawkishly observes that "No breastplate shields the heart / from injury. No armor." More often, the frankness of the homiletic imagination in these poems contrives a disarming invitation to credulity.

Characteristic of this volume at its most pleasurable is "A Game of Jack Straws," whose passages of finely wrought description give way to an even wittier form of mimesis. Using her syntax to simulate the precarious heaping-up of game pieces, the poet unearths in her game of jackstraws a type of the house that Jack built: "If you had the hammer / you could fix the stairs / that lead to the basement / that shelters the rat / that shows you his nest / where the nails are hidden." What we do not learn from this winsome poem is that the apparently innocuous site it chooses for embellishment was once distilled from the larger stage of history: from a fourteenth-century peasant uprising whose leader loaned his name to the game the poem describes, from a massive dispossession that converted tools of labor into the expedient weapons of rebellion, from a system of class hatred and fear that made *Jack Straw* a synonym for worthlessness or triviality once rebellion had safely been put down. The historical process by means of which the struggle between poverty and privilege is miniaturized and made the stuff of pastime produces a cultural trope of no small charge and consequence, but Shore seldom wrestles with difficult conversions of scale. She prefers to confine her interest, in this poem as in so many, to the context in which an object has already been set aside for contemplation, a context chiefly domestic, where the delicate counterpoise and disengagement of jackstraws in the parlor suggest nothing more remote than the delicate counterpoise and disengagement of limbs in the bedroom, "the young husband, /

who, at daybreak, extracts himself // from his sleeping bride."
There is charm in such associations, but the poem is more re-
markable for the filiations it suppresses than for those it pur-
sues. Sometimes the miniature, the prefabricated miniature, is
also a diminishment.

The issue is not merely aesthetic, of course. The favored per-
ceptual apotheosis in these poems recreates the gaze of the pre-
cocious child, a gaze we are likelier to discern in the girl child
than in the boy and are readier to admire in the woman poet
than in the man. The test case for Shore's deployment of the
childlike, and a poem that exceeds her usual decorums, is a
poem about the Jewish High Holy Days. Attending services in
her synagogue, the young persona beholds in her surroundings
a condensed history of the Jews. In the Hebrew alphabet of the
Torah she sees "stick-figure batallions marching to defend /
the Second Temple of Jerusalem." Beneath a neighbor's covering
gesture she sees the numbers tattooed in a concentration camp.
In her own sudden nosebleed she sees something like the plague
of blood that afflicted Egypt. This evolution of parallel texts has
ceremonial and historical warrant, of course, but it is an imagi-
nation heightened by heat and fatigue that finally conveys to the
child the voice of God: "*you are a Chosen One, / the child to lead your
tribe.*" And it is an only partly attributed imagination that con-
ceives the child to be "spat like Jonah from the whale" when she
walks from the synagogue "back into the Jew-hating world." Only
partly attributed, because this very weighty indictment resonates,
and is meant to resonate, well beyond its immediate context.
The lessons of history are real, and hatred is to be feared in every
casual desecration: the windows of the synagogue have been bro-
ken and its walls spray-painted by vandals. And the pedagogy of
the sacred calendar is real: the girl is taught to construe her
world as under siege from enemies. But the poet refuses to me-
diate between the history subjectivized and reprised in the mind
of a heat-dazed child and the universalized indictment vested in
the last line of her poem. She takes cover in the privileged moral
realm of the child and the embellishing preciosity of a simulated
childlike imagination, and from that doubly privileged realm she
launches the most far-reaching claim to be found in this book, a
claim to locate the real somewhere beyond the merely private. It
is a claim unreproduced and unassimilated elsewhere in *The*

Minute Hand, a claim that defies the very genres in which the poet has chosen to write, and a claim by which we may measure the problematic ethic of point of view.

Jane Kenyon, *The Boat of Quiet Hours*

The beauty of repose is a beauty most of us may only fitfully emulate or wistfully, and from a distance, behold. It is the chief beauty of Jane Kenyon's poetry and the informing ground of her vocal and speculative range. She moves, in *The Boat of Quiet Hours,* through the articulate seasons of her New Hampshire home and through the many modulations of human affection, human grief, the ceremonies of loss and sustenance. She has a good ear: the interplay of syntactical and linear and stanzaic duration, which accounts for so much of the music in free verse, is consistently well-conceived in these poems; the economies that account for so much of form seem rather to be the natural products of mindfulness and equilibrium than the more agitated record of willful poesis. The poems turn a generous and just regard to the textures of common experience, but they make room, too, for the pressures of eschatology, as when under the quotidian rubric of "Drink, Eat, Sleep," the poet's drink of water from a blue tin cup prompts a figure of transubstantiation—

> The angel gave a little book
> to the prophet, telling him to eat—
> eat and tell of the end of time.
> Strange food, infinitely strange,
> but the pages were like honey
> to his tongue

—as also in these lines from "Rain in January," which find in the local elements nature's transcription of failed prayer:

> Smoke from the chimney
> could not rise. It came down
> into the yard, and brooded there
> on the unlikelihood of reaching
>
> heaven.

As these passages testify, the other pacing in which these poems are expert is the pacing of imagination, those phrasings that are turns of mind.

Kenyon is self-reflective in the quiet of her contemplative book but never self-indulgent. Even when her perspectives are the recreated perspectives of childhood, her voice is unwaveringly the voice of an adult; it cultivates no false ingenuousness. The resourcefulness of achieved composure may be observed in the canny negotiations of "Depression in Winter," where the abstraction and imperiousness of mood (depression) are outmaneuvered by the humble "little space" (depression) that comes "between the south / side of a boulder / and the snow that fills the woods around it." This space, though small, gives wit new foothold and a chance to rescue the self from self-absorption: nice use for a pun. When next the poet acts as amanuensis to depression and must write her way out of its claustrophobia, she most subtly resurrects the transfiguring space behind the boulder and finds there a biblical paradigm. Here is the second poem ("Depression") in its entirety:

> . . . a mote. A little world. Dusty. Dusty.
> The universe is dust. Who can bear it?
> Christ comes. The women feed him, bathe his feet
> with tears, bring spices, find the empty tomb,
> burst out to tell the men, are not believed. . . .

Whatever the sexual politics here, the poem's special pleading is deftly submitted to correction by a longing for the impersonal. This reliable restraint, which is as much an ethical as an aesthetic habit and as much a matter of context as of local counterpoise, affords a useful lesson in the ways that poems may benefit from one another's company. I can think of books in which this poem would appear, and would be, small-minded. Kenyon's is no such book.

Oh, the imagination falters here and there: the self-chastening with which the poet concludes her autumn drive in "Deer Season" is too simply a scruple by rote, too like the scruple that ended the poem that came before, too flatly recorded, too little satisfactory to the mind. The unnameable longing in "Ice Storm" is at once too literally and too literarily annotated, the argument-by-allegory in "The Bat" a shade too tidily scripted. But these are minor failings and contained ones, no serious impediment to Kenyon's cumulative persuasiveness, to the sweet sobriety that fashions that rarest of things: pure song.

William Meredith, *Partial Accounts: New and Selected Poems*

The 103 poems William Meredith here renders as his *Partial Accounts* have been culled from seven previous books and more than four decades of writing. Prominent among the pleasures this body of work affords are those engendered by the suppleness and discretion and durability of its formal enterprise. Here is a poet who asks us seriously to consider the rhymed quatrain as a unit of perceptual pacing, the villanelle as the ambivalent and ritual simulation of fate, the sestina as a scaffolding for directed rumination, the sonnet as an instrument for testing the prodigious or the ineffable against the longing-for-shapeliness we know as "argument."

Time and again the most eloquent formal negotiations in this book are those of the sonnet. Meredith makes of the form a resource and receptacle for an exquisite poetic tact, a means by which the lyricist, for all his partialness and partiality, may make himself accountable, may address even the most intemperate calamity or immoderate joy without trivialization and without false puffing up. The calamity that formed the matrix for Meredith's first two books of poems was the Second World War, during which he served as an aviator in the United States Navy. Even—or most especially—for a readership brought up on other wars and other prosodic habits, the war sonnets "Carrier" and "Transport" constitute a remarkable lesson in the chastening power of decorum: it is we who are finally chastened, so safely away from the front. The war poems give way to love poems in Meredith's third book, but the sonnet takes up its familiar thematic burdens with the freshness of a reinvented form. "Sonnet on Rare Animals" addresses with sublime irreverence the very poet who made the sonnet English: the poem is at once a refutation and a reprise of Wyatt's "They Flee from Me," a sweet-and-scathing conversion of the older poet's spite into a fable of kindness-in-love, the sweeter and more scathing because Meredith lets drop no overt allusion to the predecessor whom he so outstrips in charity.

Meredith has a habit of talking back to his elders. He writes in alliterative tercets that hearken back to the very beginnings of poetry in English. He pursues in rhymed trimeter an Auden-esque intractability ("And this dark capacity / Of quiet looses a fear / That runs by analogy / On your page, in your house, for your dear") even more telling than the revisionary homage to "Musée des Beaux Arts" in "Hazard's Optimism" or the modest refutation in "Talking Back (to W. H. Auden)." He writes anatomies of trope and allusion: in a poem named for the "Simile," Meredith gives us the long-tailed figure run amok at last. The epic simile, the simile of Homer, the simile of digression-on-the-battlefield, is here all vehicle, ungrounded and unretrieved by tenor. Here even the syntax is lost, all gone to subordinate clauses, "As when a heavy bomber in the cloud. . . ." When war moves to the air, the lost quite simply fail to come home.

Among the previously uncollected poems in this volume is a sestina about "The Jain Bird Hospital in Delhi," which describes the monks and nuns who tend sick birds and believe in the interconnectedness of human and animal life. Their gentle ministrations and gentler philosophy come to seem responsible for the filiations wrought by the sestina's six end-words in all their redundancy and overlay. As in any good sestina liberally construed, the changes rung on the repeating words are themselves portentous. In the shelter of the Jain bird hospital, *prey* becomes *pray*, though it cannot shake off *victims* and *quarry*. Belief in the transmigration of souls makes for a fluid anthropology: *human beings* in this poem are interchangeably *men, women, laymen, poultrymen*, and *poor forked skyclad things*. *Violence* divides its allotted appearances with its counterpart *ahimsa*, or *non-violence*, coming out just ahead at four to three, which is about the best ratio we could hope for. Only *illusion* is constant.

Perhaps the best-known poem reprinted here is one that shares a strategy with "Simile," in that it is all, or nearly all, poetic vehicle:

> Touching your goodness, I am like a man
> Who turns a letter over in his hand
> And you might think this was because the hand
> Was unfamiliar but, truth is, the man

Has never had a letter from anyone;
And now he is both afraid of what it means
And ashamed because he has no other means
To find out what it says than to ask someone.

His uncle could have left the farm to him,
Or his parents died before he sent them word,
Or the dark girl changed and want him for beloved.
Afraid and letter-proud, he keeps it with him.
What would you call his feelings for the words
That keep him rich and orphaned and beloved?

("The Illiterate")

Rime riche and identical rhyme throughout, the word always and only equal to itself: these selfsame iterations insist upon the material, talismanic, iconic status of words, the status words must occupy for one to whom they do not habitually yield. The illiterate is, of course, a type of the poet: because he cannot or will not make words disappear into easy instrumentality, words do not lose their aura in his hands but gather into themselves a remarkable conjunction of powers and possibilities. And thus the conjunctions in the last line of Meredith's poem, not *or* but *and:* the man is rich in reverence, orphaned or unsponsored by the common, disregardful pragmatism of language use, and beloved as only the last believer shall be beloved.

Socrates tells us that the written word is an orphaned word, and Chaucer sends his litel book into the world to make its way cut off from a father. The most mature of writers—and Meredith has been among this company even in his youth—consign their partial accounts to the public domain with some ruefulness, knowing full well that the health of their children must now depend upon the comprehending collaboration of strangers. Touched as they are by goodness, rich in craft and thoughtfulness, the poems collected here should find themselves well treated by their readers if any shall, having already made themselves beloved.

Howard Nemerov, *War Stories: Poems about the Long Ago and Now*

Like William Meredith, Howard Nemerov served as a flyer in World War II. Meredith's war poems were composed in the course and the immediate wake of the event, and, though they take a mortal measure that cannot help but inform his subsequent poetry, that poetry quite naturally mobilizes on behalf of other concerns as the years go by, and the retrospective labor of bridging these transitions turns out to be no great matter of strategy: a *Selected Poems* almost inevitably defers to chronology for sequence. Nemerov's war poems, or those at hand, were written at a considerable distance from the event, and they raise very interesting questions of context. How shall a book be structured to contain them, so that other subjects do not pale before the one great subject? How shall allowance be made for what has come between the "long ago" and now? How shall those attendant features of the genre—the glamour of retrospective danger, the embellishments and obscurations of memory, the flattering and provoking curiosity of a largely civilian and culturally amnesiac audience—how shall these affect rhetorical posture and tone? "War Stories," Nemerov calls them, as one might say "a Canterbury tale," a genre whose versions of authority and augmentation we think we know something about, a genre whose subject is as much the motives and fallibilities of the narrator as the alien circumstances he describes, a genre to be taken with a grain of salt.

Nemerov could not be more coolly aware of the issues. "What Daddy did on Opening Day? Yes, well, / He led the squadron out before first light": so begins a D-Day poem called not just "D-Day" but "D-Day + All the Years." "And there I was, is how these things begin," is how this thing begins, a "War Story" written on Memorial Day, 1986. Nor is Nemerov by any means undermining the seriousness of his own project with these canny attentions to frame. The poems are moving, for one thing, and more moving because the less naive. And the subject of Nemerov's portraiture is as much the dialogics of memory (or storytelling, plain and simple) as it is the war:

> Remembering that war, I'd near believe
> We didn't need the enemy, with whom
> Our dark encounters were confused and few
> And quickly done, so many of our lot
> Did for themselves in folly and misfortune.
> ("Night Operations, Coastal Command RAF")

Looking back with a double focus to the self as a young pilot and the self as a boy who built combat planes of balsa wood and admired the pilots of an earlier war, Nemerov triangulates, thus miming the thing he contemplates, which is the manipulation of scale itself, what we commonly call perspective:

> And memory, that makes things miniature
> And far away, and fit size for the mind,
> Returned him in the form of images
> The size of flies, his doings in those days.
> ("Models")

And what about the problem of the anticlimax? How shall other experience measure up to the "boredom, fear, fatigue" of combat, the bliss of release from combat? Nemerov writes of his return to civilian life as of "The Afterlife": "The Gates of Paradise opened," he reports, "and let me out." Salvation turns out to be another exile and Paradise the paradise of expectation only, just enough of bliss to last about the length of a bus ride from Fort Dix to Newark, a train ride from Newark to Penn Station.

Nemerov's other rhetorical resource, of course, is the structure of his book. The poems described above are the war poems proper, the ones that are willing to gratify expectation while they ask us to reassess it. They are grouped together as "The War in the Air," the central of three sections, shrewdly conceived, that constitute *War Stories*. Section 1 takes its title from that other war, "The War on the Streets," the war that came between the good war and the way we live now, the war fought at home to end the war we are proud to have hated so well. Nemerov finds room in this section for poems that in a less forcefully conceived collection would be miscellany. He documents here the casualties that are part of no grand design, no war among nations, and casualties (the dead shuttle astronauts, for instance) appropriated for a grand design only by the euphemizing piety of a nation trapped in its own public relations machine. He documents, above all, the incremental casualties of the spirit brought on by what our theorists call the commodification of desire: we want what it's in somebody's interest to persuade us we want; we want to buy. Refusing to buy, Nemerov takes a very caustic look at Ronald Reagan's strong new America, from the mannequins in its shopping malls to its miracles of science. Section 3 is the quasi-Miltonic "War in the Heavens." The metaphysical boast implicit in the section title unveils a mostly rueful project: the poet keeps looking to heaven all right and to the galaxy of his intellectual forebears (Freud, Dante, Shakespeare), but the news is mostly discouraging. The poet sounds for all the world like a believer—why would an agnostic bother to be so irreverent, or so angry?—but his is not the new comfort theology. "Though God be dead, he lived so far away / His sourceless light continues to fall on us."

Reservations about so fine a book? Poems here and there ("Intimations," "At Sixties and Seventies," "The Shopping Mall, the Moral Law," "The Biographer's Mandate"), of the species of epigrammatic satire, seem to me to succumb to stridency or inertia or both. The subliminal masters here are no doubt Ben Jonson and his eighteenth-century heirs: the inevitable comparison will be to Philip Larkin. The poems I've mentioned lack the torque and formal buoyancy that distinguish Larkin's finest affectations of misanthropy, lack the temper and mobility of Nemerov's own "Ultima Ratio Reagan" and "On an Occasion of National Mourning," poems that are near neighbors in intent and in this volume.

That said, let me again praise the mind that conceived this book in all its range and knowingness. No predictable mind: when Nemerov looks through the media packaging to regard Halley's comet, that astral celebrity so recently on tour, he sees something like the flight of a sparrow through a mead hall:

> The fast and faint and temporary star,
> Dragging the streak of tail that in our comic books
> Is the artist's way of representing speed,
>
> Heads out diagonally across the field
> Of royal blue darkness with some specks of stars,
> Where, absent the beasts, the shepherds, and the kings,
>
> The unmanned universe remains, traversed
> By this ice-blue burning snowball that returns
> At the interval of an aged person's life
>
> And wastes the rest of time crossing the vast
> That separates one nothing from the next.
> Words fail us, and The Word, that failed before.
>
> ("A Christmas Card of Halley's Comet")

C. K. Williams, *Flesh and Blood*

For three books now, C. K. Williams has been working in the long, commodious, flexible lines that have come to be his trademark. Even the byways of typography are part of the face by which his readers know him: not even the exaggerated proportions of an oversize book (Houghton Mifflin tried one in 1977) can keep these lines from extending to wraparound. Lines-and-a-quarter or lines-and-a-third produce the rhythm we see on the page: some prodigal, loquacious overspill that is rather a kind of second wind than the syncopated part-lines of enjambment. Williams has restricted his line to octaves in the new book, and what other eight-line poems in the language would prompt one to praise their orchestration? The formal proposition is all but oxymoronic. But orchestration is the genius of this book: multivocal, richly textured, finely scored.

The capaciousness of the line is matched by a capaciousness of spirit in *Flesh and Blood*. The poems are didactic fables, documentaries, confessions, indictments, portraits, billets-doux: and the list of exemplary instances would virtually reproduce the table of contents. One might have expected the eight-line restriction to produce a kind of semantic and perceptual uniformity after a while, especially in poems so committed to process (here must be the rising action, here the discovery). But the poems gain latitude from their very numbers and proximity; the cumulative pressures of interrogation and scrutiny free some poems for the simpler tasks of lyric description and vignette, though simplicity is always relative in a poetry this fertile. And, page by page, the poems cease to be mere integers: together they constitute a strenuous, changeable, divided, and impassioned essay on the moral life of urban humanity.

One of the ethical tests to which Williams submits himself and his readers with some regularity is the test of flagrant disclosure. He will not turn his eyes away (or not soon enough) from the beautiful woman's artificial hand, from the young boy's deformed legs, from the car-struck dog and its frenzy of pain, from the manifold, mutable, resourceful means human beings have devised for visiting harm upon one another. He will make us flinch and make us behold our own flinching. He is especially uncompromising on the species of cruelty we direct toward children (see "Will," "Easter," "Good Mother: The Metro") and the radical critiques of adulthood that may be read in the play of children (see "Artemis," "War," "The Park"). He renders the vulnerabilities of the aged in such a manner that all of us may know just how far our love for them falls short and may know what we ourselves are in for ("The Lens"). He records the casual indignities of life in a dying civilization and the spontaneous moments in which a dying civilization may behold itself in the mirror of allegory:

A much-beaten-upon-looking, bedraggled blackbird, not a starling,
    with a mangled or tumorous claw,
an extra-evil air, comically malignant, like something from a
    folktale meant to frighten you,
gimps his way over the picnic table to a cube of moist white
    cheese into which he drives his beak.
Then a glister of licentious leering, a conspiratorial gleam, the
    cocked brow of common avarice:
he works his yellow scissors deeper in, daring doubt, a politi-
    cian with his finger in the till,
a weapon maker's finger in the politician, the slobber and the
    licking and the champ and click.
It is a lovely day, it always is; the innocent daylight fades into
    its dying, it always does.
The bird looks up, death-face beside the curded white, its foot,
    its fist of dying, daintily raised.
                                                        ("Greed")

The final section of *Flesh and Blood* comprises a prolonged elegy to the poet's friend, Paul Zweig, who died in 1984. As the sequence moves from the description of Zweig's final days to speculation about the afterlife, from the recitation of shared, habitual pleasures to homage and farewell, even as it documents considerable reservoirs of feeling, it seems to me to suffer from a kind of airless confessionalism. In meditations addressed directly to his dead friend, Williams itemizes for that friend the course of his last illness, the conditions and aftermath of his death, the "ambivalences and withdrawals" in his marriage, his insecurities as a poet, and, in much detail, the stages of grief among his survivors, especially this one survivor, the poet Williams. The second-person address sadly neglects decorum in such circumstances, though it has been chosen, and violated, out of love. And the inventories seem to me to lack some third dimension, some vehicle like those so manifest in the earlier sections of this book. This sequence so thoroughly paraphrases its own preoccupations that there's nowhere else for the mind to go. Not that one would wish ungratefully to restrict the discursivity of Williams's work. One of the great accomplishments of that work, one of the great functions of its commodiousness, is the escape from overly tidy formulations about the nature of figurative invention. The shape and pacing of explanation have figurative force, as much as do synecdoche and metaphor. If the schemata of classical rhetoric endorse a proposition by making it seem to echo the symmetries of the universe, the masterfully regulated digressions, ellipses, and overdeterminations of an apparently casual rhetoric, like Williams's, may propose their own shapes for cognition and cosmos. It is not discursivity per se that confines this elegy to a flattened premise; it is perhaps the poet's very reluctance to release his friend, even so far as to distinguish figure and ground.

John Hollander, *In Time & Place*

Conventional wisdom has it that reading Milton is either very safe for the contemporary poet, because Milton simply has no direct bearing on the projects of late-twentieth-century poetry, or very dangerous for the contemporary poet, because Milton's language so colonizes the imagination and is so patently inappropriate to the projects of late-twentieth-century poetry. Very safe or very dangerous, the author of *Paradise Lost* is in either case impossible. And yet two very considerable recent books of poetry have derived their major lineaments and momentum from this impossible forebear and, far from compromising either music or personality, have in consequence augmented their investment in the here and now, which is to say, in both the resonant accidents and the rigorous ideations of time and place. In *The End of Beauty*, Jorie Graham pays homage to *Paradise Lost* in both her overarching subject—the expulsion from scenes of closure and our consequent relegation to this perilous, mortal meantime, with all its radical indeterminacies—

and in her chief method—the syncretic survey of classical and Christian paradigms. In the very shrewd format of *In Time & Place,* John Hollander compiles an allusive florilegium—one hears the echoes of Spenser, Marvell, Boccaccio, and a host of other literary voices—but it is Milton's etymology of exile, Milton's celebration of domestic love, and Milton's Garden that are of deepest structural significance. Fully half the poems in Hollander's book derive their subjectivity, and their daily labor, from a marriage lost. The other half revive a venerable tradition by contemplating the expulsion myth as a theory of language. In between, and called "In Between," is a section that theorists of influence will have expected to find in any book that has so opened its heart and ear to the supreme and overbearing literary monument of the seventeenth century: a simultaneously self-effacing and self-asserting anti-monument written in the form of a disappearing journal.

The poems "In Time" are written in what Hollander calls "four-by-fours," or tetrameter quatrains, rhymed in "mirrored halves," or *abba*. The poet lifts the passage of time to legibility by means of a strict, even a confining, form. Insofar as time is also the thematic preoccupation of these poems—and it is—it is the time of loss. The poet grieves in form and in public over what is itself a matter of form, a form that exists precisely at the juncture of public and private, the form we know as marriage. Although these poems propose quite charmingly "to rhyme" the missing partner "back to bed again," the more realistic anxiety expressed in "mirrored halves" is that the face in the glass shall reveal itself not as the responsive other but as the entrapped and longing self, the self turned back on itself by a blind eye or a stagnant pool, the self that paralyzed Eve at the water's edge before she found her generative self in another ("The Looking-glass of Grief"). The poet speaks quite readily, as this poet has always done, about his own formal motives, constructing in his quatrains at least two explicit defenses of rhyme and one capsule history of the *abba* stanza in English: the last of these measures time not only in iambs but in the accretions of poetic tradition. "Having lost you, I'd rather not / Be forced to find my way as well / In the broad darkness visible / Of prose's desert." Expelled from conversation in the Garden, the poet may at least find consolation in the company of his eloquent elders.

Form is spatial, of course, as well as temporal: modern physics has taught us that there's no such thing as time without place, and the little room of the stanza is as good a place as most from which to negotiate our subjection to the ephemeral. Among the many cultivated witticisms deployed by Hollander in *In Time & Place* are those pertaining to cultivation: his diachronic stanzas have a landed pedigree. They are plots of earth; their lines are furrows; georgics are the sport of an urban and an urbane mind. On the serious side—and Milton's example is always also serious—Hollander evolves a poetic of longing from the twin metaphors of husbandry and husbanding, the two domestic labors, which are love.

The linking document in this book is a playful and obsessive narrative that as willfully erodes the distinctions between time and place as it does the distinctions between inside and outside, figure and ground: it makes a metaphoric mongrel. Its pages, for instance, are said to be chambers, which mysteriously infiltrate the territory of metaphoric tenor and are eventually said to be like pages. The lubricant for this fictive "In Between" is a disappearing ink that seems to have been made from the old confessionalism: tears, sweat, a "fine white wine," "remembered rain." When the words disappear, the writer is freed both of and for overriding egotism. When the words return, as they begin to do in the course of the narrative and as they must have done if we are able to read them, they launch their return with an uppercase *I*. Riding on its own melting, this purported journal publishes both the death and stubborn resurrection of the author.

The poems of "In Place" are prose poems, written in formal complement to the tight stanzas of "In Time." And, as if to defy, once again, the false distinctions of binary opposition, these poems are of a musicality that surpasses anything else in the book. As one has come to expect of Hollander's poems, these speculate with remarkable mobility about their own conditions of production. In "A Week in the Country," Hollander writes an anti-*Decameron*, in which narrative dies of self-consciousness. In "Keepsakes," he writes about the narrative aura that attaches to lyric fragments and about words as they progressively separate themselves from use or reference and become pure icon.

Indeed, the overwhelming subject in these poems of "place" is the relationship between words and things. The poems are shadowed by that old dream of language, the one without contingency, the one in which words constitute pure access to the nature of things, the one of Adam naming in the Garden. "It is as if every word here were embracing the object it named" ("In Place of Body"). The dissolution of this dream is exile from the Garden and the face of God: now everything that grows can be heard to sing, "*ô Mort*" ("Crocus Solus"). To which the poet has commonly replied with praise of what is mortal. Robert Hass praised "*blackberry, blackberry, blackberry*" at just such a juncture ("Meditation at Lagunitas"). Hollander posits a crocus: "One flower points to nothing but itself, a signboard bravely hung outside the signpainter's. . . . A sign? O, more." Death (*ô Mort*) is the mother of beauty (O, more). Because meaning, since the expulsion, can never be a system of fixed equivalences but is rather the momentum of our longing for lost plenitude, the disjunction of signs and things in no way bodes the impoverishment of meaning. Hollander imagines "In Place of the Body" a garden of "absent forms" whose gestures are "as if," a garden where "meaning would flourish, whether in absence or presence being of no matter now."

Hollander's poetry is not much interested in the anecdotal lives of humankind. Its heritage is an uninterruptedly high-cultural heritage. It would rather smell of the lamp than of the alfalfa field or the subway. For all its subtle overturnings, which is to say, by means of them, it manifestly endorses the canonical schemes and topoi. There will be those who find it temperamentally uncongenial. But readers of any temperament will also find that *In Time & Place* bountifully exhibits and repays attention—of how many books can this be said? And the poems of "Place" would be sublime in any context.

7

Plenitude

Richard Howard, *Like Most Revelations*

Richard Howard has published a tenth book of poems: limber, literate, jubilantly crafted, wry, and, above all, densely peopled. The poems are chockablock with male and female, the famous and the less so, the living and the dead, the largely or fractionally fictive, persons summoned back from obscurity or from East Hampton for imagined conversation, revelatory vignette, mock-chronicle, dramatic or epistolary monologue, posthumous satire, lecture, romp. Howard uses the persona as other poets use metaphor or memory or grammatical period: as the foundational unit of meaning and imaginative play, the formal occasion for stricture or hypothesis, the ruminative vehicle, the rhetorical premise. He do the moves in different voices.

He is nothing if not self-aware. In a poem called "Writing Off," Howard extracts an *ars poetica* from the exemplary pairing of (1) a contemporary poet much noted for his elegant austerity and (2) the lavish graffiti covering an empty lot in East Los Angeles. "'In a field I am,' our latest laureate / divulges, 'the absence of field.'" The laureate Howard cites (no longer our latest—apotheosis is fleeting in democracies) is Mark Strand; the lines are from a famous poem ("Keeping Things Whole") in a famous volume (*Reasons for Moving*). Howard's "latest" is a bit unfair, quite apart from the revolving door of latter-day laureateship: the poem in which the poet "divulges" (perpetual present tense) is several decades old now, and the poet's performance of self has altered over the years. But let's grant the present poet his point. Strand's virtuosity has always had its grounding in absence: the vacated plotline, the deadpan sub-

First published in *Poetry* 167, no. 5 (February 1996): 287–99.

lime, the mail-order trappings of affect, the first-person pro-
noun bereft of ingratiating idiosyncrasy. Strand has never sited
poetry within the adjectival clutter of human affairs. Howard, by
contrast, by temperament, by choice, makes the "converse
claim" for plenitude. The opposition he adduces, and exempli-
fies, is a rich one:

> Now
> behold the field from which Mark Strand
> proclaims himself absent: here is a wall
> and at its base a ruined car
> filled with spray-cans that strew the ground as well,
>
> and every inch of wall and car and ground
> is covered, cancelled, *encrusted*
> with the spirit-writing known as graffito,
> cursive abuse, cacography
> which by its very glut becomes glamor,
>
> a collaborative chaos of uncials,
> illegible and thus elect.
>
> ("Writing Off")

This poem, among its other illuminations, offers a wonderful
meditation on the nature of authorial signature. The excre-
mental virtue of inscription on the wall, car, and vacant lot re-
veals chiasmus at the heart of self. The *amo* cut into a tree trunk,
the *ergo sum* spray-painted on a gutted Chevy, the *Johannes fecit*
chiseled on cathedral stone, have this paradox in common: the
flattest self-assertion pays frankest tribute to that which exceeds
it. The self is a self because it wants, is wanting, and must clamor
for attention. And the excess—the graphic surfeit—that impairs
one sort of legibility engenders another:

> How many times we must peruse
>
> these depths before the deepest impulse floats
> to the surface and is legible:
> the inenarrable FUCK which appears
> only after the eye has long
> frequented more decorous instances.

Write off: to cancel, as in a ledger, by making the complementary, or "double," entry. Written off: aggressively dismissed (and oxymoronically embraced as a rejected intimate), as in "Fuck you." Writing off: riffing on.

Howard slyly names his chosen agonist just when that name (Mark Strand) will sound most like the (self-asserting) autograph it is, a kind of writing on the sandy margin. Strand's name, like Strand's poetic, foregrounds the collusive nature of inscription and erasure, fair ground for comment in a poem (Howard's) that celebrates the friable face of urban graffiti. "Now / behold the field from which Mark Strand / proclaims himself absent." "Proclaims": the absence Strand performs and Howard explicates is open exhibitionism. In that it resembles the fecund impersonations of Howard's own poetic mode. These two past-masters of epideixis, the poet of absence and the poet of plentiful presence, have in common a knowing ruthlessness about the serviceable gestures and performative construction of self.

What becomes, then, of the opposition that gives "Writing Off" its impetus and argument? Howard exuberantly hawks the here and now, the then and there, the *literal*, in lieu of the abstract. And he makes forcefully clear why literalism has never been the sport of lesser minds, nor the default epistemology we at our peril take it for: the overscripted "empty" lot in East L.A. does not exist, we learn at last, except in a snapshot described in a poem. Its redundant materialities—the objects of use recruited as canvas, the layered graphesis, the snapshot, the poem—press the letter so hard it becomes spirit again, press self-assertion back toward anonymity, toward the mystery of community and that to which community refers. "All participation in art is based on the existence of others," writes Howard (quoting Hebbel) in the poem's epigraph. Rightly construed, the empty lot is ceremonial, "an unvisitable shrine" whose "obscure artisans," like the artisans of Luxor and Lascaux, can teach us "to approach the divine." Saving the genuine grandeur of this proposition from grandiosity are Howard's urbane conflations of high and low. He writes a book in which the momentous (revelation) and the quotidian (like most) are interanimate. He also writes—and powerfully argues for—an irreducible dialogic: counterbalancing the commemorative snapshot (graffiti in a West Coast slum) is the cover illustration on the present book. Gorgeous, highbrow, spare, abstract: it is a recent collage by the poet's friend Mark Strand.

A final note on Howard and community: among the more remarkable exhibits of unblinkingness in these poems is their workaday engagement with catastrophe. AIDS is everywhere in this book, as it is everywhere in the communities—artistic and intellectual, urban, gay—to which this book most commonly refers and addresses itself. AIDS is the interlocutor, the next of kin, the goes-without-saying, the extra place at the table, and even—hilariously—the natural misconstruction, as when the poet's friend mistakes a Mozart quintet (K452) for a next-generation AZT (in "Culture and Its Misapprehensions I"). We have our languages for devastation. But how are we to conduct ourselves when epochal horror becomes a usual suspect? It is a piece of bravery to acknowledge—to *perform*—this challenge to candor, to character, to tact.

Margaret Gibson, *The Vigil: A Poem in Four Voices*

Margaret Gibson endows this poem with a novelistic reach. Set on a single autumn day in 1986, *The Vigil* tells the story of a family whose losses (a young child's death by drowning, willed separations and amnesias), labors (the making of homes and of "livings," the observation of seasons, domestic nurture), and collaborative negotiations of shame and betrayal (a father's alcoholism, an illegitimate birth, the thousand attendant alibis and secrets) now resonate through three living generations, represented in this poem by four women: a grandmother, her daughters, and a grown grandchild. The poem takes its title and its dramatic occasion from the annual gathering of these women to tend the firing of a wood-fueled kiln that belongs to the potter among them. Tying its considerable narrative commitments to a quasi-Aristotelian unity of time and place, the poem also ties its considerable affective and expository labors to the vehicle of interior monologue. And therein lies the structural impasse.

For Gibson seems not to have anticipated the tonal and pragmatic consequences of her chosen narrative mode. Interior monologue may have myriad promptings—a scraped knuckle, the sound of a fog horn, a moral or psychic dilemma—but it has by definition no rhetorical *occasion*, which is to say, no audience except the necessarily unacknowledged one. It is one thing to inform the reader that a character watching over a wood kiln "shudders awake" and to invest her watching with the significance of "vigil." It is quite another to require that character to narrate—and to no one—the actions she performs as she performs them and to provide the solemn vocabularies of import. "From dreaming," the poem begins, "I shudder awake . . . I haven't kept / this vigil well enough. . . . glowing chars . . . seem runic . . . I watch my hands tremble . . . I think of . . . I want . . . to atone." The distribution of consciousness among four characters in eponymous sections rather multiplies than ruptures the unalleviated interiority. Events transpire, revelations occur, and characters intersect, but nothing may be rendered without the swaddling of first-person present tense. "I want," "I know," "I stoke," "I stack," "I grumble," "I laugh," "I brood," "I feel," and, always, "I remember." Sarah cannot comfort an injured child without narrating how "the dark of my breasts / and shoulders settles / over him." Lila cannot bake bread without describing "the simple work of kitchen ritual." So it goes when the central actors in a tale must dress the stage and run the lights and provide symbolic embellishment to their own unfolding plotline.

Much of the constraining task is strictly informational. When nineteenth-century playwrights had a lot of filling in to do, they'd open with the servants discussing the affairs of their middle-class masters. Gibson's monologists must manage on their own. So two of them begin the day by recalling the decades-old death of a child and a father's habitual immersion in drink, and each must summon these scenes independently (their musings are interior) and must do so well before breakfast (the story has miles to go). The resultant problem is not so much implausibility—a reader may justly be asked to grant a certain portion of psychological and poetic distillation—but airlessness. Four women inwardly rehearse the cruxes of a shared lifetime. Four women divide the symbols of the hearth (and its fissures) among them. Four women are systemically denied even the slightest reprieve from self-absorption. "I move," "I pause," "I hear," "I rise," "I shiver," "I murmur," "I breathe." Gibson has condemned her heroines to endless autobiography.

The irony is that a poet who clearly values and means to cele-
brate the salvific and semantic powers of plain craft and daily
labor should have stranded herself with so little honest labor to
perform. Her poem is bound to a double affliction: an over-
reverent mythic valorization on the one hand (of the sort that
made many women impatient with the psychologizing strains of
first-wave feminism), and a disingenuous pragmatic project on
the other (her four personae must perform unremitting histori-
ographic and expository roles while affecting the associative in-
directions of inward rumination). Meanwhile, that wonderful
workaday business from which language derives nine-tenths of
its meaning—the address to *someone*, real or imagined, hated or
loved, manipulative or misapprehending—the workaday busi-
ness goes begging.

And more's the pity, for Margaret Gibson is capable of some-
thing very different. When she describes a daughter washing the
body of her dying father, she writes with eloquent restraint.
When she allows herself some indirection and lightness of
touch, her angle of vision is fine and new. Here is a mother re-
membering dinnertime when her children were young:

> Bart sailed bread cubes
> over the surface of his soup. Sarah made
> stories from her blue willow plate—
> birds changed back to lovers,
> a house floated like a flower
> beneath a bridge, around the world
> to China, where someone needed succor,
> needed her potatoes—I'd given
> her too much to eat.

Phrasing, metrics, the fairy tale spun and sweetly co-opted: every
lovely rhythm works. Such moments are more rare in *The Vigil*
than they ought to be, their rareness a direct result of the con-
ceptual and formal miscalculations that pervade the poem.

Jan Heller Levi, ed., *A Muriel Rukeyser Reader*

Muriel Rukeyser (1913–80) was a writer of capacious imagina-
tion, broad social and intellectual sympathies, articulate political

convictions. She had little patience with the sequestrations of lyric voice the twentieth century has offered up as its sorry tribute to Romanticism. Jan Heller Levi has compiled a "Reader" that honors the full range of Rukeyser's remarkable formal and intellectual enterprise: in a single book, we may read excerpts from eleven volumes of poetry (Rukeyser published seventeen in her lifetime), the introductory chapter to her biography of Willard Gibbs (1942), extensive selections from *The Life of Poetry* (1949), five songs from the stage play *Houdini* (1973), a lecture delivered to The Academy of American Poets, eight sentences from an interview in *The New York Quarterly,* and two difficult-to-categorize, politically impassioned excerpts from a 330-page fantasia on the life and times of Wendell Willkie, Republican candidate for president of the United States in 1940. The composite form of this last-mentioned sourcebook—part verse, part prose, part biography, part social history, part manifesto, part parable—makes its title, *One Life,* overtly polemical, a salvo in Rukeyser's lifelong campaign against the conventional partitionings of thought and action.

The best-known portion of Rukeyser's published work—her poetry—retains pride of place in *A Muriel Rukeyser Reader,* but, far from quiescently "contextualizing" the poems, this book proposes a radical rethinking of genre and discipline. In Rukeyser's hands, the lyric opens its stanzas to physics and folk song, to journalistic interview and congressional deposition, to nursery and briefing room, to sick room and the stock report. She brings to prose the poet's aptitude for image, the journalist's aptitude for narrative, the teacher's tactful aptitude for complex information and hypothesis, the child's unparalleled aptitude for discomfiting candor. She brings to analytic and expository labors a demystifying curiosity—a *believer's* skepticism—about the foundations and structures of knowledge. She brings to social activism an uncompromising eye for the savage differentials of cultural and economic privilege and an equally uncompromising conviction that art is not a luxury commodity but a necessity for the sustenance of human life and human community; on the picket line and at the podium alike, she is remarkably free from self-congratulation.

Rukeyser's *Theory of Flight* won the Yale Younger Poets Prize when she was only twenty-one. Like first books everywhere, it features a "Poem out of Childhood." Quite at odds with the common run of first books, this one is "out of" childhood for real: fully fledged, tough-minded, mindful of its grounding in that which came before. For the young Muriel Rukeyser, barely out of Vassar, seems never to have labored under the notion that the world ought somehow to contract to approximate the dimensions of self. The self she had to work with was always *in* the world, made of and for and by the world, and determined upon a reciprocal remaking. Not for her the facile oppositions between poetry "public" and "private":

> Sappho, with her drowned hair trailing along Greek waters,
> weed binding it, a fillet of kelp enclosing
> the temples' ardent fruit   :
>
>   Not Sappho, Sacco.
> Rebellion pioneered among our lives . . .
>
>   Prinzip's year bore us   see us turning at breast
>   quietly while the air throbs over Sarajevo.
>   ("Poem out of Childhood")

Rukeyser did not abandon Sappho, as the sensuous "turning at breast" alerts us; her books abound with the fleshed, emphatic love of women. But the life of erotic longing and evolving domestic allegiances was a life of other urgencies as well: Sacco and Vanzetti are put to death in Massachusetts, black men are hung from trees in Alabama, West Virginia miners breathe, then fail to breathe, with silicon-ravaged lungs, a Serbian nationalist (Gavrila Prinzip) shoots the Archduke Franz Ferdinand in Sarajevo.

Rukeyser was six months old when the archduke died and Europe came apart at the seams. The principle of personal and historical and intellectual shaping she attests to in these early poems ("See us turning at breast / quietly while the air throbs over Sarajevo") is one she explicated all her life, *consulted* all her life as a template for prosodic and rhetorical shaping. What she renders once in an elegant line and a half, she renders again, with no diminishment of force or clarity, in the ampler byways of prose narrative. The introductory chapter to Rukeyser's biography of the physicist Willard Gibbs is one of the glories of the present anthology. (It is Gibbs [1839–1902] to whom we owe the Phase Rule, a pivotal contribution to the early history of thermodynamics and "one of the most celebrated and beautiful laws," writes Rukeyser, "of theoretical physics.") Bent upon the lineaments of one man's mind and its luminous questions, Rukeyser begins her book with the story of a slaveship mutiny in 1839. Her pretext? Eighteen hundred thirty-nine was the year of Gibbs's birth (as hers was "Prinzip's year"); the captured mutineers were held for trial in the university town where Gibbs was born and would spend his career; his father eventually played a role in the legal disposition of the case. Her argument? The urgent deployments of human curiosity, of science, of linguistics, of compassion and morality, are one.

Josiah Willard Gibbs, the father, was a philologist and professor of theology at Yale. Forty-two Africans, including three small girls, were lodged in the county jail at New Haven, pending trial in Hartford. At issue was whether they ought to be tried for murder and piracy, restored as property to the men who had purchased them in Havana, transferred as salvage to the ship's captain who had rescued their foundered ship off Montauk, or granted freedom according to international treaty and national law (they had in fact been imported from Sierra Leone after the 1817 Decree of Spain made such trafficking illegal). The Africans spoke a dialect no Spaniard or American could understand and thus were unable to testify on their own behalf. Enter (it's the county jail) Josiah Willard Gibbs. He held up one finger, two fingers, three; made phonetic transcriptions of what he was told; went down to New York harbor, boarding ship after ship, until he found among the cabin boys and sailors two who recognized the words for one, two, three; brought them back as translators to Connecticut. The Africans' case was ultimately argued, and won, before the Supreme Court of the United States by the aged John Quincy Adams.

The slave ship and the philologist. The shared material project of Icarus, da Vinci, Orville and Wilbur Wright. The Spanish Civil War, which she covered as a journalist. The silicon mining scandal, which she recorded in "The Book of the Dead" and made the searing centerpiece of her second book of poems. The labor organizer Anne Burlack, the composer Charles Ives, the rabbit in the basement at the Rockefeller Institute. "The rabbit, its great thrust and kick of muscular pride, as it was carried under the fluorescent lights, where against the colored unbroken skin glowed the induced cancers, fluorescing violet." The scene is from *The Life of Poetry*. It is not about the scientist's insensitivity to animal rights, though it is, in a sense, about animal rights. And about the fearful cost and moral imperative of seeking out new paradigms, a cost and an imperative that science and poetry share. The researchers "were no longer looking at cancer as a fact, an isolated fact. They were taking another approach: they were dealing with cancer and the body on which it fed as one thing—an equilibrium which had been set up, in which the cancer fed on the host. One could not exist in this state without the other in that state. It was the relationship which was the illness."

Like any good scientist, Rukeyser respected her tools. The early poems are rich in prosodic experiment: internal rhyme and slant rhyme, modernist abutment, adapted folk and high-cultural forms, aural/visual syncopations. The social satire is wicked and tender and exuberant ("The Village was never like this in the old days, / throw a brick down the street and you'd hit a female poet"). The supple stanzas fairly shimmer with intelligence. The portraits of and provocations to feeling are formidable. "Three Sides of a Coin," "The Lynchings of Jesus," "More of a Corpse than a Woman," "M-Day's Child Is Fair of Face," "Fog Horn in Horror": all of them written before she was thirty-five. She respected the tools and their history, but her measures are never simply received: "Did you think this sorrow of women was a graceful thing? / Horrible Niobe down on her knees: / Blu-a! Blu-aa! Ao."

I confess I find Rukeyser's later lyrics less compelling by and large. The broader strokes are meant to have the force of distillation, but the lines are commonly blander, the moral more predictable, the portent forced, the outward gaze at once less comprehensive and more categorical. Despite many fine poems and portions of poems ("The Conjugation of the Paramecium," "Despisals," "St. Roach," to name just a few), the world Rukeyser delineates in the 1960s and 1970s is a smaller world than the one she makes and inhabits in the 1930s and 1940s. It would be wrong, however, to make too much of these diminishments. Why should we ask, except that we, too, fear aging and mortality, that a writer's best coincide with her latest? The best of Rukeyser is enough to stop the heart. We owe Jan Heller Levi considerable thanks for reminding us on what a scale a first-rate mind may work.

Alice Jones, *The Knot*

Alice Jones completed her early professional training in internal medicine and is now a practicing psychiatrist, an affiliate of the Psychoanalytic Institute in San Francisco. We learn these facts from the thumbnail biography on the jacket of her first book of poems and, in a different, more extensive sort of detail, from the poems themselves. The book is structured with considerable thoughtfulness. The first of its three divisions confronts with rage and grief and rueful self-scrutiny the death, from AIDS, of a once-intimate friend. The sequence is written as a kind of double helix: the story of premature death (the friend was only forty when he died) intertwining with the story of emergent sexual and affiliative subjectivity (the friend and the poet were early lovers, when the identity-conferring habits of desire were as yet, in part, occluded and the poet all too ready to construe herself as the-one-who-is-unable-to-capture-his-longing). The extratextual grounding of this personal history is of course beyond the reader's ken; retrospection, with its consolidating, sense-making inclinations, and the inherent structures of language, with their suasive provisionality, make any autobiography an exercise in "as if." This book encourages its readers nevertheless to regard the key events and personae described within the poems as "real," which is to say, as the durable ground of moral and affective authenticity. Alice Jones is a writer for whom story—the shapely, textured story of the self-in-the-world, the self-in-the-body, the self-in-key-human-relations— serves as the primary bearer of meaning. And who better than a psychoanalyst can tell us about the power of story to produce the self?

It is in the second section of this book that the author's psychoanalytic training surfaces most explicitly. The poems here contemplate what is still sometimes referred to (and not neutrally, as feminism has pointed out) as the pre-Oedipal phase. The absorbing relationship Jones renders here—the cosmos she renders—is that of mother and child, before that cosmos comes to be mediated by the father. The drama is that of first division: splitting chromosomes, the divergent gestational heartbeat, the birth-expulsion. Jones's celebratory theme, her object of wonder, and her argument (even, at times, her quarrel) is the irreducible *embodiment* of human consciousness.

Body is the frontal theme of section 3, whose centerpiece, a twelve-part poem entitled "The Cadaver," traces a medical student's progress through her gross anatomy course. The progress is inward, along the paths of dissection, epistemological and professional indoctrination, and psychic revery. The student, rendered throughout as *you,* is brought again and again to the cognitive precipice where inner and other converge, where the body inhabited as continuous "self" meets the body dismembered and acted upon, the body in its eloquent thing-ness. The *you* has some unfortunate rhetorical consequences (the poet is perpetually telling this other one how "she" thinks and feels), but it makes a kind of mimetic sense as well. The first person narratively distanced by the grammatical guise of the second person, who acts upon a third (distanced in turn by death and scalpel and formaldehyde): the drama of pronominal case reproduces the drama of consciousness, the palpability and elusiveness of personhood, or being-in-place.

It will be obvious by now that the title of this book aptly reproduces its structure. Thematically, its three parts intertwine, circle back upon one another, make a complex unity out of multiple strands. The argument of the poems is also, and feelingly, for connectedness, not merely the formal connections of poetic shaping or synthetic imagination, but the elemental and generative connections between one person and another, between, for lack of better terms, the body and the mind. The knot in this book is credo.

And credo derives its intensity from risk: it is not founded in bland certainty but in discovery and precariousness. Hence its nearness to petition:

> Send rain, down to the dry bare bones of me,
>   the tarsals planted in sand, no sage
>   or mint or parsley will grow here, snails
>   are sucked dry, leave frail shells
>   in the dug garden's dirt, no flowers no fronds;

Send rain, down to the deep bowl of my pelvis,
        barren red hollow, the empty sack
        sags now with age, the scarred yellow ovals
        discharge their eggs in irregular cycles,
        no longer linked so well to the moon;

Send rain, down to the restless quartered meat
        that thuds on my ribs, whose valves
        measure thin blood as it seeps through
        the pipes feeding desiccated organs,
        whose mortal work forms sludge;

Send rain, down to the small transparent curve,
        the opaque lens that filters dim light
        to the lustrous surface and on to dense
        convolutions of brain, the task of my sighted
        vitreous globes that turn in their padded cells;

Send rain, down to the knots and whorls
        where memory continues to pile its thick layers,
        sloughs surface, and roots reach into
        that grey ground where my neurons grow sparse
        and leached soil sprouts nothing new.

Send rain.

                                                    ("Prayer")

Having cited the author's formidable best, however, I must
also report her failings. "Prayer" is not a representative poem. De-
spite local bright spots and careful intertwinings, the general run
of writing in this book is less than dazzling, on both technical and
conceptual grounds. By way of getting from one place to another,
for instance, the author relies heavily on the fallback ligature of
first-person, present-tense, interior narration: "I think of," "I
imagine," "We envision," "I picture." She tends to summarize
every psychic discovery and spell out every moral. Her dangling
modifiers, her confusions of *like* and *as,* convey not plausible
transcriptions of colloquial speech nor stream-of-consciousness
but lapses of attention and technique. Most damaging to the con-
ceptual project of this book is the omnipresence of Freudian
cliché. The title sequence of *The Knot* is, alas, a series of womb
poems. Their immersive materiality is often quite wonderful;
their interpretive motions are disastrous. The womb as first

home, the womb as paradisal garden, the womb as suffocating coffin: these figures simply will not serve as poetic discovery; they are shopworn; they are silly; they are, in the bad old sense, received. Psychoanalysis has been and remains one of the great intellectual adventures of the twentieth century. It serves the discipline poorly to use it as a source of ready metaphors.

Alice Jones is a writer with a subject and, clearly, with considerable resources. If we may judge from the prominent placement of "The Prayer," she also knows her own best work when she beholds it. The superb poem with which the present book concludes promises a body of powerful writing to come.

8

Among the Wordstruck

John Ashbery, *And the Stars Were Shining*

Heather McHugh, *Hinge & Sign: Poems, 1968–1993*

If ours were a more reverent country than the one they gor-
geously exemplify, John Ashbery and Heather McHugh would
long ago have been made to endure the title of national trea-
sures. For the treasure we too long and belligerently have taken
for granted—our fractious, healing, double-dealing, on-the-
make vernacular—is nowhere so richly turned to account as in
the poems these two have been bestowing upon us for years.

And the Stars Were Shining is Ashbery's sixteenth collection of
poetry: fifty-eight shining new lyrics. We've come to expect the
dazzle by now, the deadpan shifts from speed to languor, the
jocular abutments of idiom, the teeming fluidities of tone.
Much of the fun derives from the poet's affable penchant for
verbal slumming: the down-market colloquialism ("the upshot
of it was"), the off-tempo platitude ("Take care of values. The
rest is shopping"), the willful solecism, the loopy archaism
("caitiffs," "knickers"), the klutzy pronoun ("One reads how an-
other one's kinsman / has inherited a vast estate in Scotland. /
The things that happen to other people!"). This is serious fun,
of course. Take the pronoun: an article of speech we prefer to
regard as transparent, expeditious, an unobtrusive item of use,
pointing with the least amount of ruckus to a subject whose re-
peated proper naming would be too heavy on the ear. And sud-
denly this pronoun becomes a problem: thumping, shifty, el-
bowing its way to center stage. Ashbery's *one* rebounds on the
perpetrator, hilariously foiling his effort at decorous locution by

First published in *The New York Times Book Review* 99, no. 43 (23 Octo-
ber 1994): 3.

exposing its subtext of pipe dream and envy: saddled with "one," he'd rather be "other people," and rich. Likewise Ashbery's *you*, who is now the reader, now the self, by turns the beloved, the place holder, the mere rhetorical subject, the res publica, the pushy, democratizing handshake of American speech, as in "you wouldn't want to be seen in there" and "your typical big business scam." Two parts social satire and one part metaphysic, Ashbery's pronouns force us to look again at the tenuous boundary between *one* and another, you and me.

As in the work of Ashbery's estimable forebear Wallace Stevens, these fluid pronouns are part of a larger provisionality. The hoped-for, the at-our-backs, the contrary-to-fact: "what I call the subjunctive creeps back in." We are (have you noticed yet?) contingent here. The message is mortality, but the feeling is not gloom. Our narrow purchase in the world turns out to be just ground enough for the salutary, celebratory, home-building work of imagination.

I have scarcely begun the inventory of habitual Ashbery amusements: the passing come-hither ("nine busboys to be bussed—er, tipped"), the deflationary echo of grandiosity ("I see, I read, I nap"), the homage by way of rejoinder (as when William Carlos Williams's "No ideas but in things" becomes "No ideas in things, either"), the thousand companionable pleasures of a mobile wit. These poems are perfect in their pitch, savvy in their metric and changeable pace. And in this, its fifth decade, John Ashbery's resilient body of work is astonishing most of all for its sheer (the poet will not feel flattered at first) good nature. The poems are supple, skeptical; they puncture our tenderest complacencies, our carefullest phraseologies; they show us for the rubes we are. But what might easily have been an exclusionary aesthetic is instead, and durably, invitational. Here, in its entirety, is "Myrtle":

> How funny your name would be
> if you could follow it back to where
> the first person thought of saying it,
> naming himself that, or maybe
> some other persons thought of it
> and named that person. It would
> be like following a river to its source,
> which would be impossible. Rivers have no source.

They just automatically appear at a place
where they get wider, and soon a real
river comes along, with fish and debris,
regal as you please, and someone
has already given it a name: St. Benno
(saints are popular for this purpose) or, or
some other name, the name of his
long-lost girlfriend, who comes
at long last to impersonate that river,
on a stage, her voice clanking
like its bed, her clothing of sand
and pasted paper, a piece of real technology,
while all along she is thinking, I can
do what I want to do. But I want to stay here.

The key to this remarkable career appears to be a genuine ca-
paciousness of spirit. Learning without pedantry, copiousness
without glut, facetiousness without the sneer: gifts to thank our
lucky stars for.

While Ashbery is a virtuoso of the sidelong, Heather McHugh
has gamely favored the frontal assault. For her, too, meaning is
a form of motion. For her, too, words are the stuff of seduction.
But McHugh is all type A: impacted pun and riddle and high-
jinx, the fractured jazz of the logo-motive universe. McHugh has
spent her literary life in devout refutation of Saint Paul: no
spirit but *in* the letter, her poems proclaim. And very high spir-
its they prove to be. McHugh loves the thingness of words—
their heft, their shimmy, their slickness and burn—she is a
shameless fetishist. And one who knows her lineage too, as wit-
ness, for instance, "The Woman Who Laughed on Calvary":

I saw what good

comes to; I saw the figure
human being cuts, upon its frame.

. . . What I got
of humanity there
was the hang

This poem, among the generous gathering of new work in the
new and selected *Hinge & Sign*, is homage to Samuel Beckett (a
presiding spirit in many of the older poems as well, though

McHugh suggests in her preface that the likeness may have been unconscious for a decade or two). The word made mortal flesh was always Beckett's profoundest joke, the one we entered in the middle of, the one on which we never got to vote. The hang of the human, the body of God for agnostics: McHugh can't help but fill her mouth. And though the thing she celebrates is not exactly eucharist, it's something very like it. Death weaves its cell at the base of the spine, and what can we do but praise it? Joy and terror pitch a single tent. McHugh writes her elegies and her love poems from a single, sexual source.

This wonderful book isn't flawless. The six-page "Scenes from a Death" could have used a bit of ruthless cut and paste. The sequence titled "32 Adults," which began as a collaboration with the visual artist Tom Phillips, seems a little out of balance on its own, unmoored from the collages with which it is still in (ghostly) dialogue. And in disparate poems, the proportion of effort to yield goes slightly awry at times, as when McHugh refuses to choose among prefixes: "If History is ported," she writes "(com, re, pur)." Bent-out-of-shape is one of this poet's nimblest moves, but "com, re, pur" is straining pure and simple.

But look how it's done when the thing's done right: "Sebastian's Mirror" is a poem about the burden of self and, as I take it, a shimmering gloss on a favorite Shakespeare comedy. Remember the one where the Duke is in love with love? And the lady in love with her mourning? And everybody self-absorbed, until two shipwrecked twins distract them into outwardness? *Twelfth Night* makes a moral of the letter. Malvolio becomes its dupe because he can only read by the light of self-aggrandizement. McHugh (because she loves it) rescues the letter for use, unlocking its secret as only goodwill (*Ben-volio*) can do:

> Behind her eyes,
> behind her back what do
>
> you see, as she admires the mirrors?
> Everything so long
> mistaken for oneself
>
> is there: a breath of h's,
> sleep of z's, and two that end
> in eros . . .

(67)

McHugh's our laureate of physical love. Her poems about sex are poems of poetic vocation. In her marvelous "I Knew I'd Sing," the nascent lyricist finds her voice in a childhood venture at vulgar slang: the word was Anglo-Saxon for the female genitalia; the punishment was a mouthful of Ivory soap. "But still / I'm full of it," she writes, and "knew / from that day forth which word / struck home like sex itself." Saint Paul had better take cover. Even God, this word-struck celebrant insists, is nailed to the physical world: "without / material, he has no act."

9

Unequal Seas

Dennis Schmitz, *string*

Dennis Schmitz's subjects are the ones all poets write about: mortality, desire, the ripening of speech. Schmitz's purchase on these subjects is such as to make us know why we cannot do without poems. The poem gives a face to life that would otherwise escape us, unrecognized and unreclaimed. The poem is a *string* that marks a path through generality, which would otherwise engulf us. The images that govern this volume are those the poet assembled three books ago: the river and its analogues (piss, milk, ditch water, vomit, sweat, soup, semen, drool); the river and its spawn (fish, island, swimmer, tongue). He has lived with this gathering as with a shopful of familiar tools, and they turn out masterful work. From "the poet at seven":

> what is the word
> the tongue evolves to? already the hands
> are solo when he draws
> the two-legged sheep in his account
> of heaven. already he can lift
> his head from its print
> in dreams & soon he will learn
> the eye, even when released
> into sleep, is just a fish the steady
> river forms.

What is idiosyncratic in Schmitz derives not from his avoidance of inherited figures, but from his persistence in them. Thus, the linking of husbandry and conjugal love in "delta

First published in *Parnassus: Poetry in Review* 8, no. 2 (1980): 210–28.

farm." The unremitting alliance of bed and landscape accumulates new pressure behind an old conceit:

> a friend weighs little a wife
> makes the body heavy
> as she swims away in the marriage
> sheets—she seems more
> strange than my mother's
>
> face surfacing
> in memory. so the drowned
> displace the living—
> not my wife's but
> mother's thirst dries the sweaty
>
> fingerprints
> from the handle of the short hoe
> or cutter
> bar skimming the overflow
> our salty bodies deposit between
> windrows. together we pressed
>
> drool from the sugar
> beets & threw
> or wished to throw our bodies
> like pulp to the few
> hogs we kept for meat on the tufted
> mud of an upstream
> island. this is the sweetness we refused
> one another.

Peculiar to this poet is an unsettling democracy of the imagination, an absence of metaphorical hierarchy. What we would in another setting call tenor and vehicle are here allotted equal persuasiveness. There's no mere literal setting, geographic or emotional, to retire in the guise of pretext, no analogue to serve as mere embellishment. This is itself a kind of immersion technique; we cannot exert control over the figure by consigning one of its branches to secondary status. Note the steady rhythms of displacement in the passage above: the woman's thirst attends the speaker from bedroom to field; saltwater overflows from river back to the body's delta; the windrows return us to field, and the drool to bodies, until we know its source in the fruit of the land; tufted mud just resists becoming tufted mattress. The syntactical moorings of *overflow* and *drool* run counter to their purely semantic affinities. By the time we reach the following stanzas, the poem's two scenes, the bedroom and the river farm, compete with equal magnetism for *beds* and *sheet:*

> when women visit
> they only fix cots in fallen
> down coolie shacks below
> the town produce
> sheds now abandoned & shifting
> with the sun's weight.
> when they leave boys
>
> will lie restlessly
> fishing in the narrow
> beds skiffs make, between the pilings
> hear the sheet
> metal pop nails to trail
> in a swifter river.

The image displaced advances its argument in the very act of bringing forth a counterpart: "so the drowned/displace the living." Saltwater backs "miles / inland to preserve / what it kills"; so the foreground image does homage to its predecessor, which will become its inheritor. There is no escape from the other and, for the reader, no escape from the labors of imagination.

The metaphorical technique is corroborated by Schmitz's development of the period and the line. Suppression of the uppercase, which in the hands of a less scrupulous poet would register as mannerism, here sustains the larger poetics of immersion. The authority of the full stop is undermined; phrases are moored as much by echo and proximity as by syntax; the little fortress of the sentence opens its gates to surprise:

> our daughter crawls
> through fever one week
> then her mother the week after
>
> dies. my wife,
> still my wife, what I have
> of you, this residue, this love-

salt, will not let me cross private
places in my body
anymore.

Avoiding both correspondence and counterpoint to the phrasal units, lineation parcels out the time in which the poem may do its work. The eye moves from right to left not where the syntax calls for pause nor where resistance would establish a beat, but as though the object under examination were being turned in the hand. The informing rhythms are not primarily those of the speaking voice, but those of the comprehending mind. This is subtle music, the cultivated burden of song.

Quibbles. An occasional over-clotting, as in the beginning of "soup":

a fistful
of spinach or chard sleep will make
a garden, & hidden snails that dying whistle

as the bunch opens, boiling: cautery.

At the end of "making a door," in which the speaker builds a doll-house with his daughter, a baffling lapse into portentousness:

I go on distributing
myself over the assigned parts.
the house is almost done.

I hand her the saw.

And rare cases in which the imagistic graft fails and remains superimposition:

even the face is a navel
transplant which never

takes root.

Burlesque, if that's what is meant, can be a useful instrument for testing the limits of obsession; at a certain reach, the image exhausts consent. Schmitz is seldom at his most limber when the poem begins to mock its subject or its own methods. When, as in "navel" above, he finds his tone by testing the waters of excess, the approach tends to blur the tone he finds. In "planting trout in the chicago river," however, the error, and the joke, precede the poem; the original, the inimitable Richard J. Daley of Chicago, as notorious for his malapropisms as for his old-style city machine and his outsized villainy during the 1968 Democratic Convention, seems to have lost his hold on slippery words again. The epigram he has inadvertently turned on himself, the Gospel "fishers of men," also serves as epigraph to the poem in which he is commemorated:

> aldermen & ethnic reps can help themselves

> to rods as he bends
> over the awful garbage, as his lips let go
> this fish rehearsed four nights
> in which his tongue grew

> scales, the Gospel epigram hooking
> his mouth both ways
> until he talked fish-talk
> but still hungered for human excrement.

In this case, the poem finds a way to embrace the double-talk it might simply have ridiculed, or been stranded upon. The final stanzas expand into a fine exegesis of the humor we call black:

> in turn each of us

> will have to learn to cough
> up fish, queue from Lake St. Transfer
> at the river to disgorge
> & after, wade at eye level

> under Dearborn bridge, intuitive,
> wanting flesh, wanting
> the warm squeeze & lapse
> over our skeletons because the fin repeats
> fingerholds, the gills
> have an almost human grin.

The technical and conceptual resources of Schmitz's poems are usually, and impressively, allied in a single cause. The dispositions of line and sentence defer closure and release the elements of syntax in a steady unfolding. Figures steer a demanding course between equivalent, equally valent, poles. The relentlessness of experience provides both subject matter and a moral stance; the implicated eye may no longer posit the discreteness of its objects:

> our thought-
> out acres of orchard high
> ground where picking ladders descend
>
> legless into their own
> reflections.

The tongue is formed by speech:

> to be is to be raised
> from mother flesh plural,
> to love distinction but be some part
>
> of travail that summers
> in an older body. Sara's grandmother
> speaks as she walks
> the sunburned orchard holding Sara:
> these are the limits
> & so is the way you repeat
>
> them. you
> drink this truculence; if you don't
> choke you are healed.

Most striking in this book is a cumulative authority of image. The figures are just, not because they confirm some common pictorial imagination, but because they elicit a deeper, more disturbing recognition. Schmitz can endow an adjective with the force of epithet:

> 6 pm sun
> condenses on the unequal sea.

He can lodge necessity in an oxymoron:

> the maculate purity of flesh.

He can explicate affinity:

> so the drowned
> displace the living—
> not my wife's but
> mother's thirst dries the sweaty
>
> fingerprints
> from the handle of the short hoe
> or cutter
> bar skimming the overflow
> our salty bodies deposit between
> windrows.

We had not known we knew that the drowned have a powerful thirst, and now we cannot forget it. They drown because of thirst, and then they thirst for the living. Before and after conspire on a single proposition. So it is with understanding. A poet like this can teach us to see before us with the eyes of memory.

Thomas Lux, *Sunday*

As Virgil describes him, the poet cultivates a necessary idleness. Thomas Lux has named his new book for the day of rest, and has seeded it with thumbnail portraits of the artist as virtuoso idler, minutia's most avid scribe, supreme purveyor of the capacity for play:

> Somebody says: We're all in this together
> and we board the lifeboats
> in this order: first children, then poets,
>
> then men and women fighting
> it out.
> > ("Poem Beginning with a Random
> > Phrase from Coleridge")

The rhythm is a sort of smart-ass syncopation:

> Suppose you're a solo native here
> on one planet rolling, the lily
> of the pad and valley.

You're alone and you know
a few things: the stars are pinholes,
slits in the hangman's mask.
And the crabs walk sideways
as they were taught by the waves.

("Solo Native")

Technically, the poems are very polished, good at what they do:
a jazzy talk line plays itself out against the counterpoint of line
break and abrupt caesura. Conceptually, cross-patterning oc-
curs between two strains of affection: the poet/persona pays
homage to the discrete objects of attention, the world's sharply
etched trouvés; he also delights in and insists upon the quirks of
imagination. The danger in the one pursuit is preciosity and, in
the other, a kind of sheer claim for the privileged sensibility.
The poet's wit wards off such dangers with fair constancy,
though the savvy, almost wholly implicit undercutting of his own
pronouncements is not so much a sign of modesty as a pre-
empting of would-be detractors.

A subtler danger than those above is that the objects of vi-
sion, those points of resistance to the clever self, will be all too
easily co-opted. In his previous full-length volume, *The Glass-
blower's Breath,* Lux was wont to employ the luminous detail as ar-
gument, a move with which to clinch a poem. This is "History
and Abstraction":

The dates carved on bridges
and public buildings—1932, 1951,
19–, and so on: bland

abstractions, bland history.
I like to face history
and abstraction with a positive

condescension. Here's the facts:
technology reached its peak
with the electric chair, nature

poets can't enter the forest
without weapons—this is the truth.
The inexorable boredom of history,

The flat kiss of abstraction . . .
But why do I insist it's too late
to refuse permission

to operate? It's not, it's not
irrevocable, my flesh
is not weightless!

—And, I can be glad, glad
for the small plane of skin
beneath this woman's chin,

and glad for the dead
glassblower's breath still caught
in the red vase behind you.

The poet, of course, has no intention of doing without either history or abstraction. Elsewhere he owns and adheres to "my favorite abstraction, desire." The ploy has rather to do with representation. The better part of history is its record in artifact, the vase where once the glassblower breathed. The better part of abstraction is concrete detail, abstracted from context or explanation, lifted from the woman to whom it once belonged. Desire is best known, if not fulfilled, by its objects, in synecdoche. The parallel strategy in *Sunday* moves poems toward a final reverberant image:

I want you, spider: walker-on-the-ceiling,
creeping black thumb.
Here's my forehead, the pad
or your landing. So slip
down your rope, that purest advance
of saliva, settle close
enough to my lips.

I'll know what you know,
thank you. Exhort, tell the story
of the eight-leggers. Put your fur
next to mine, relax down here
on the pillow. You look like a priest
in a multisleeved cassock
so let's confess

to each other: We're beasts,
twelve limbs between us,
sharing one house, the same desires
and industry: to design
the web, live on what we catch
from air, and always returning,
always, to the spun eluctable cave.

("Spiders Wanting")

There's no more resisting this image than there was the breath
in the vase; Lux is a journeyman of delight. What strikes me as
problematic about these poems, however, is the extent to which
they're content to be setups for their own best (and conclud-
ing) lines. I'd like to see the poem that begins somewhere in the
middle of the third stanza above.

Upon occasion, Lux has extended the duration of voice, and
the differences are substantial. *The Glassblower's Breath* concludes
with a long, ten-section poem called "Almost Dancing." Again
and again in Lux's work, we are meant to infer the uncertainty,
even the panic, on the other side of bravado. In the second
poem in *Sunday,* the speaker expects a sparrow to land on his
porch before dawn: "The lower half / of her beak will be miss-
ing, / she can't eat, / *and* she is still alive." In a later poem: "It's
really a slingshot we lie in / thinking: hammock." Precarious-
ness, the staple of human existence. Lux's solo native is always
strange to the world, always on the verge of extradition, always
beset with allergies to the native element, "like a simple vase not
tolerating water." And danger is the enabling condition of
speech. The subject can name the wall he leans on when it
threatens to collapse. In "Almost Dancing," the informing bio-
graphical circumstance is a serious bout with "bum lungs." What
lifts this poem above so much of the rest of Lux's work is not
some naively construed "authenticity," not some scraps of "real
life" thrown out to the prurient reader, but the sheer duration
and resulting complexity of voice. To be sure, the poet allows
himself a certain apparent directness:

—Always the blades of the pinwheel in my chest
are sharp and spin with the wind of each breath.
—Always in my green mansion in the wind
the place between my head and the pillow is calm

and I love best the scalpel moving away,
the scalpel moving away I love best.

But this is only one among many notes with which he extends his range. What is elsewhere scrupulously left implicit begins in this poem to take on specific life: it is that which bravado is poised against. And more: the coincidence of peril and opportunity receives a fine and moving explication. The singer sings *because* he has too little breath.

Another ten-section poem, "Flying Noises," occupies the final pages of *Sunday*. It does not ground the volume in which it appears as "Almost Dancing" grounds *The Glassblower's Breath*. It does distill and forge ahead with the technical project of the book, illuminating as it must the relation between methodology and subject. The method is paratactic in the extreme. The poem is faceted, each section at an angle to adjacent ones. Only the smallest units of ellipsis and bonding are registered with punctuation marks; the hyphen and the apostrophe alone survive a general banishment. Syntax inverts; the units of sense abut. One of the faces the poem puts on is that of a love poem. "There's the various positions in which we exult":

Once gone like gloss in a flashflood
Once an animal loving another of another species
Once one joyful crumb of the fully individual
Once a convict dreaming of mowing a hayfield
Once an avenue upon a bench sits one moment of present
Once under deep enough to ring the literal sleep-bells
Once the dead changing shirts in their small booths
Once farmers merely bored by drought
Once all the birds invented as toys
Once the heart-angles the trillion u-turns of blood
Once the flying noise

Ovid refers to the various positions in lovemaking as *figurae*. The posited single creature, the union of perceiver and perceived, the one sufficient word, has only a figural representation. Adjusting the intersecting angles of approach is a project without end. No day of rest for the lover or the poet.

The fourth section of *Sunday* comprises work "from *Orphic Songs:* Versions of poems by Dino Campana." Four of the seven poems, however, were among those published only after Campana's death in 1932; the remaining three appeared in *Canti Orfici*, which the Italian poet published in 1914. Lux makes no reference, either in his text or in his acknowledgments, to I. L. Salomon's *Orphic Songs*, but he appears to have consulted freely the one book-length selection of Campana translations currently in print in this country. A poem Campana's posthumous editor entitled by its first line, "*O l'anima vivente delle cose*," is named by Salomon after an internal phrase, "I, nailed to a boulder," and by Lux, "Campana, Nailed to a Boulder."

"*Poesia facile*" is a sonnet in the Italian; Lux takes more liberties, both formal and substantive, with this poem than he does with any of the others and makes a case, I think, for "versions" of this kind:

> I don't want peace. I can't endure war.
> The world walks through me in a dream—
> I'm silent, can't sing, I'm lonely,
> Lonely but for my dear and ruinous songs.
> —The mist filling an enormous harbor,
> That's what I'd like.
>
> Yes!, an enormous harbor
> Crowded with velvet sails,
> Ships undulating and anxious to lift
> Anchor and head for the blue
> Horizon, where only the lisp
> Of the wind slips by in perfect hues.
>
> And the wind carries these hues
> Forever across oceans.
> —I'm dreaming. Life is lousy
>
> And I'm lonely, almost.
> O how am I going to get out of here?
> O when will my heart, stupid and trembling,
> Wake up blind to the sun
> The endless sun?
>
> ("Just a Poem")

The poet walks through the world in Campana's poem, not vice versa, and he's alone, without qualifiers. The "but for my dear and ruinous songs" and the "almost" are new. Salomon's more literal rendering of the final stanza goes like this: "O when O when in a fiery morning / Will my soul, free and trembling, / Awaken to the sun, to the eternal sun." (*O quando o quando in un mattino ardente / L'anima mia si svegliera nel sole / Nel sole eterno, libera e fremente.*) Lux has effectively reversed the movement here, and reminds us that "loyalty" is a complex course of action. He has decided that the stronger part of Campana's voice, or the part that appeals most strongly to his own, is that of the erratic, thin-skinned celebrant, the lusty complainer, the inconsistent iconoclast. He has bolstered this Campana with wryness (a quality that receives clearer warrant in some of the other poems) and has sacrificed to him the other Campana, the unchecked romantic with his trembling soul. The perpetrators of "versions" ought always to be sobered by such ornaments as the eighteenth-century "improvements" of Shakespeare and Lowell's upholstered "imitations" of Sappho. But this "almost" is winning, at once a brag and a flippant unmasking. This cousin to Campana is adroit.

The products of poetic "translation" must locate themselves on a broad spectrum of aspiration: the crib means only to serve as a guide through an original; a particularly remote successor may acknowledge "inspiration" in its title, in an epigraph, or not at all. The translator who opts for versions or imitations wishes to make clear his allegiance to the new poem, its coherence and proportion. One question that remains in my mind is whether these versions of Campana are more interesting in themselves or in juxtaposition to their originals, indeed, to the prior translations upon which they draw. In "Campana, Nailed to a Boulder," the poet addresses his art:

> Be for Campana a beacon, and for you
> I will carry an offering
> Beneath the unknown curves
> Of the sea.

These unknown curves are *infrenati archi* in the Italian, "unchecked arches" in Salomon's rendering; *frenata* refers to the action of braking. The more literal translation is arguably the more interesting single phrase in this instance. However, and this is what intrigues me, "unknown" is a suggestive gloss upon "unchecked," asserting as it does the indissoluble bond between limit, or hindrance, and knowledge. The function of a beacon in unknown waters is clearer than in unchecked waters, certainly, but the change is perhaps too successful a tidying up without some hint of the predecessor it elides. The question is simply whether poems of this sort are most advantageously set in the midst of the translator's own most recent poems, whether they don't seem out of focus there. The advantage of the facing-page format is that each partner in the dialogue gets a voice.

Cynthia Macdonald, *(W)holes*

The epigraph to Cynthia Macdonald's new book is a quotation from Diane Arbus; this is partly the poet's claim to lineage. The freak has been featured as a persona and a performer in both of Macdonald's previous books, but a full half of *(W)holes* involves the conscious exploration of the poem as sideshow. This poetic receives its most persuasive embodiment in "Francis Bacon (1561–1626; 1910–) The Inventor of Spectacles, Is the Ringmaster," where the poet's predilection for puns is more subdued than elsewhere, though hardly in full abeyance. If Francis Bacon the Renaissance scientist and Francis Bacon the twentieth-century painter are avatars of a single principle, incarnation is itself a kind of pun. *Spectacles* aptly summarizes the central conflation upon which the poem turns: the spectacle of bared deformity is a lens with which to focus point of view. Three sections compose the poem, each a sort of figurative overkill, a synecdoche personified; these sections are: All Mouth, All Ear, and All Eye. The poet locates the fetishism latent in synecdoche and uses it to bait a seduction poem:

> There was a lot of argument about its sex.
> Experts said, "Female, that's obvious,"
> But when it stuck out its tongue to show what it thought
> Of experts, some changed their minds and said,
>   "Androgynous."
> All Mouth did not care what they said;
> It would eat anything.

This eroticism of the grotesque presses the connection between discomfort and titillation. The curious experts, and the curious reader, engender more than they care to acknowledge. Temporal sequence alone forces us to assume that the uncomfortable tumescence All Mouth develops is the material result of outside prurience:

> All Mouth's pregnancy was difficult.
> It did not like to sunbathe
> Or swim at the pool or beach;
> It was embarrassed about the bulge of its bag.
> But it needed water all the time, needed immersion to
> Cool.

The much-noted derivation of *grotesque* from *grotto* suggests that unearthly appearance is precisely that which we would see consigned to the earth, hidden from view. On the stage and in the poem, a subtle decorum links exhibitionism to reticence:

> [I]ts kin knew that displaying
> Your triple hump or the fountains in your aorta or
> Your elephant skin or your star-spangled vulva in the sideshow
> Did not mean you could bare it outside.

Meanwhile, the reader has been made complicit. The conception, with the disconcerting obligations it entails, is meant to comment upon its intellectual counterpart: conceive for a moment of what's beyond you, and you author it. All Mouth gives birth "to part of what it lacked."

All Ear, too sheerly receptive to realize its phallic ambitions, begins a frustrated masturbation "using its own stirrup," and from this springs All Eye, the third generation, fully blown. The sideshow, the necessary obliquity of desire, the function of peripheral vision in the creation of point of view, the relation of part (and absence) to the whole, all are given their wisest reading in the final stanza of this poem. This is Macdonald at her best:

> The eye is the most courageous organ because, in a sense,
> It must always face itself. It lies in its moist socket,
> The pot of seeing, and never says that what it sees in dream

Is less than what it sees. Image and imagination,
Those eyes indivisible.
In the deep of my eye, I see
To the edge of self (all those translucent pronouns)
And beyond into the dark quarter of the circle.

In "Celebrating the Freak," Macdonald traces by means of a
pun the blossoming of secrecy into publicity:

The freak leaves us	bereft, forcing a little
Mutilation somewhere	to set things right
To wreak	penance
To set	the freak flags flying.

Whether this represents the poet's deft calculation or a happy
accident preserved, the *pennants* in *penance* have the force of a
genuine discovery, the derivation of carnival from guilt and
fear. More characteristic are the puns below. From "Burying
the Babies":

He begins with a lift and jerk and becomes the latter
When he heaves up that three-hundred-and-fifty-pound
    woman,
Vomits her all over the crowd.

From "The Lady Pitcher":

Will she win it all now or will this be the big bust which
    She secures in wire and net beneath her uniform.

See also "Florence Nightingale's Parts," from the leering double
entendre of the title to its predictable reiterations:

O comb, my comb,
My honey, my hive, but only
The cocks can stride into battle.

It is worth rehearsing here the grounds on which a pun may be
"bad," even for those who delight in conspicuous manipulations
of words. The rich doubleness of language undermines linear-

ity whether we like it or not, after all; those projects of syntax and ordered contemplation that rely too heavily upon prim exclusion will inevitably founder. If wordplay is the dialogue of intentionality with its opposite, a tactical duel with prodigal meaning, a tapping of stored, inherited semantic wealth, it is an exercise worthy of a poet. But there is such a thing as a bad pun: the pun that is an act of bad faith, a short circuit meant to elide the very powers it pretends to celebrate.

The title of Macdonald's book is the third in a willful series: *Amputations, Transplants, (W)holes*. We deduce both that the author has pursued a single, conscious aesthetic and that she has very little regard for the inexplicit. The parentheses, like an elbow in the ribs, direct us to a series of paraphrases: What are here intact, creative artifacts were torn from the body of the self, amputated, transplanted into the realm of art. As to the heart, and half of the newest book is devoted to poems of the heart, its very longing for wholeness or union with another leaves it riddled with holes. As to synecdoche, the part that serves as a whole more ardently pursues artistic consummation (is very likely to join a circus) because of its absent faculties. The major proposition about poetics appears to be this: that the relationship between poems and their source is an inverse or complementary one, that what is embodied in language is not what is proper to the speaker. W. S. Merwin's *The Lice* and Sandra McPherson's *Radiation* frame similar propositions, but they do so obliquely, by means of the epigraphs from which they derive. Their method is one among many that seek to preserve not coy enigma but the independent suggestiveness of words. A name must do more than mean with a vengeance.

A great proportion of Macdonald's most insistent cleverness has been aimed at relations between the sexes. An innovative heroine in *Amputations* finds her profession in a name she's been called; this "real ball cutter" fills her freezer "with rows and rows of / Pink and purple lumps encased in Saran wrap." The newer poems have elected another tone, but flattest irony carries on the work of boldest burlesque. As the double title predicts, "Remains—Stratigraphy:" trusts very little to its central metaphor: archaeology's stratum here is strictly surface; the poem is a retrospective addressed to one who is not so dear as he was:

1979: Taps.
Music of ice cascades to the pavement.
You write: I hope you are well.
Nails of ice puncture water, merging with it;
A stratum cannot be assigned.
Reflections of stone tattoo the surface.
Whatever the object was,
Nothing remains.

The long, final poem in this book, called "Burying the Babies," might well be called "The Mistress's Complaint." From sources as varied as Leonardo's letters and Louisa of Tuscany's memoirs, the poet stitches together another, quiltwork version of the sideshow, the story of the woman on the side. Roughly three principles govern the entry of source quotations into the poem: some reflect, or are made to reflect, in a general way upon the life of men and women together; thus, a book on the Japanese puppet theater outlines the conventions that distinguish male and female puppets, an Emily Dickinson poem levels highly acerbic charges against the institution of marriage, and Leonardo's letter on armaments to the Duke of Milan is recruited for anatomical innuendo and allusion to the war between the sexes. Some sources comment in particular upon the mistress's situation; thus, Louisa's account of abused ladies-in-waiting. Others afford the reader glimpses of plot, the scenes of assignation; Louisa's passage on court dinners introduces the lovers in a restaurant; dialogue from an Alfred Hitchcock film recalls the time they watched television in bed. This third group, of course, does service in the metaphorical realm as well: the consumption or postponement of meals refers us to spiritual hunger; food is purchased or cooked as a material bribe; failed recipes spell out failed happiness.

A punning recurrence of individual words reinforces the thematic patchwork. What is on one page an Indian curry is three pages later an attempt to curry favor. A six-page progression from all-day suckers to honeysuckle to suckling makes clear that the original all-day sucker is woman-with-child. Occasionally, the punning contributes a certain puzzle-solving momentum to the unfolding plot: in a scene designed to evoke a grade-B war romance, the lover is called away by his service; two pages later it's an answering service; later yet, the lover turns out to be a physician. Occasionally, the images are woven with a light enough hand to preserve some pleasures of discovery for the reader: a dozen pages after the mention of "polished brass scales, their rounds like suns," the image reenters through rhyme; children on a beach admire "the contents / Of their pails. And the sun shines on them like brass." More often, the featured performer, the juggler with words, guards every inch of center stage. Nor does the recurrent vocabulary reveal obsession. The portrait is not of figures or sounds that impress themselves upon consciousness but of a will that manipulates figures and sounds.

On a parallel plane, only one of the poem's sources, *The Puppet Theater of Japan,* retains real multivalence. The others, made to work for the most part against their original grain, can only seem camp. A few are treated with strictest condescension.

What is all this apparatus for? The poet unleashes irony; her persona unleashes reproach. And unleashes reproach and unleashes reproach. For twenty-seven pages the story unfolds, reducing the world around it and every borrowed book to analogue or foil for a single plaint. The mind of the poem contracts to avoid the most grievous irony of all, that language may indulge the heart's dramas as well as transform them, that, untransformed, even the dramas that pinch as sharply as death may not make a very interesting poem. There is a sort of bitterness that makes the eye hawklike on its own behalf and extinguishes all points of view beyond the edge of self. The discrepancy here between the poetic machinery and the discoveries it makes is large.

In "The Secrets of E. Munch," Macdonald imagines the symbolist's tortured canvases as an effort to disguise the soul of a sentimentalist. Under her own canvas tent, the self endures a certain amount of sardonic display, that the circus acts, like the puns, may be more perfectly rigged. Behind the barker's megaphone is the unmistakable voice of sentiment, a sentiment that uses wit for license as well as for camouflage. The sentimental self has lost in sinew what it's gained in protection. This serves neither poetry nor the intelligence, considerable in the present case, that produces it.

10

God's Concern for America

Charles Wright, *Zone Journals*

The ten "journals" that constitute the body of this book make a single formal and epistemological case, a case that has long been emerging in the larger body of Wright's work. Their case is for immanence, the deferred material presence of truth; for permeability and open-endedness; for the liminal, where eschatology incorporates the risen body of the past; for rehearsal, which is the only performative mode of consequence; for the invocatory, which is the antithesis of the iconic. The rejection of closed form in these poems is by no means the rejection of the artifactual: in Wright's theater of imagination the lineaments of human manufacture or poesis chronically bleed through the scrim of nature. The blue jay moves "in a brushstroke." Cloud banks are "enfrescoed still / just under the sky's cornice." The poetic project is always and already implicit in the observable world: "lightning bugs / alphabetize on the east wall."

Constituting nature as the threshold of speech, the poet locates a prior authority for his own ruminations, making nature the underwriter for poetry's speculative line. In weaker gestures, the circle of self-reference may smack a bit of self-endorsement ("Somewhere out there an image is biding its time"), the scene perpetually short-circuiting to the literal scene of writing. But the double inscription Wright aims for is a project of considerable stature and high seriousness, nothing less than a one-man reparation scheme for the old breach between nature and culture. Endowed with memory and aura and the fracture lines that betray what escapes us, the found world and the made

---

First published in *Poetry* 155, no. 3 (December 1989): 229–39.

world coalesce around a single longing for transcendence ("The not no image can cut"). Wright's tutelary spirits are manifold and indifferently, studiously drawn from the double realm: a turkey buzzard, a Renaissance courtier, the Blue Ridge Mountains of Virginia, the wheel that broke upon the faith of Saint Catherine, the squirrel on a power line, the ghost of Glenn Gould, the philosophic principle and the geomorphic contour known as Occam's razor. In its reciprocal, recuperative production of the past, *Zone Journals* is near kin to "Tradition and the Individual Talent," but in Wright's version of Eliot's imperial hopefulness, even landscape is part of the mutable, vested inheritance that is reformulated by every major act of imagination. Thus of Provence, seventy-seven years after the death of Cézanne, the present poet writes: "Still these colors and pure arrangements / Oozing out of the earth, dropping out of the sky / in memory of him each year."

Wright's journal poems cultivate a number of interrelated semantic and syntactical predilections. Language vamps in these pages, preferring to move sidelong into assertion, preferring the dilations and solicitations of the noun phrase and the musical phrase over the franker lineups of subject and verb. Language spins a line that lengthens from margin to margin and frequently breaks. It is a line that Wright has favored and refined for several years, a line of great suppleness and lyric beauty, a line that pays due deference to the white surround. It is a line obsessively thematized and theorized in the present poems, a line that trains itself to analogues, to fishing lines trolled through the waters of the Pacific Northwest, to the virtual lines of Morandi, Picasso, Cézanne, and the no-line of Rothko, to the "sure line the mockingbird takes / down from the privet hedge," to the generic "line" or ironized narrative lure of the "true confessions" that lend one of these journals a title. The line is the line that first divided one element from another, the line Creation spoke, the "line between sleep and sleep." The line is the trace of its own extinction, "nobody here but me / Unspooling to nothingness, / line after line after latched, untraceable line." Finally, the line is mortality's knife edge, dissecting the impermanent coils of flesh, that we may, as a character in Webster says, be put back into the ground to be made sweet:

—November pares us like green apples,

                        circling under our skins

In long, unbroken spirals until
We are sweet flesh for the elements

                    surprised by the wind's shear

Curling down from the north of Wales
Like Occam's edge to Steeple Aston and Oxfordshire.

The economy of hypothesis that modern science derives from William of Occam equates truth with elegance: maximal explanatory power and minimal fuss. In a landscape Occam's edge is the mild outcropping of prehistory. In either instance, beauty accommodates the ineffable to human sense.

In America, in the shadow of the year 2000, we are not much trained to expect of poems bright shootes of everlastingnesse. Charles Wright might yet reform us. It is the business of his poems to conceive transcendence by means that forestall it. He writes mortality's alibi:

From my balcony, the intense blue of the under-heaven,
Sapphiric and anodyne,

                    backdrops Madonna's crown.
Later, an arched stretch of cloud,
Like a jet trail or a comet's trail,

                  vaults over it,
A medieval ring of Paradise.
Today, it's that same blue again, blue of redemption
Against which, in the vine rows,

                  the green hugs the ground hard.
Not yet, it seems to say, O not yet.

Tess Gallagher, *Amplitude: New and Selected Poems*

Tess Gallagher's earliest instincts were those of a fabulist, and the contours of fable, or narrative-in-a-clearing, continue to inform her more recent poems, even those most conspicuously grounded in the clutter and wash of experience. From the beginning, she has made parables out of the dramatized self and its doubles (a kidnapper, a shadow, the nascent breasts that divide a girl from her brothers), and this dramatized self forges large-scale unities of method even as the poet moves from isolate and universalized paradigms to the increasingly explicit contexts of autobiography. The "I" is unremittingly present in Gallagher's new and selected work, set upon the stage of the poem as its chief poetic figure, embodying one portion of poetic consciousness ("I dance / like a woman led to a vault of spiders"; "I went to you in that future / you can't remember yet") and speaking another ("Time to rehabilitate your astonishment, I said / to myself and plunged on / into the known"; "I was suited more to an obedience / of windows. If anyone had asked, / I would have said, 'Windows are my prologue'"; "I think I said some survivals need / a forest. But it was only the sound of knowing"). "The sound of knowing" is bread and butter to these poems, which prefer sensibility to sense. The "I" here, as even random excerpts would make clear, is treated very tenderly by the hand that writes; this "I" loves the drama of gesture and temperament and above all loves publicity.

Gallagher uses performative or dramatized means of assertion—phrases cast as the speeches of a shadow persona—as a kind of vatic license: she can play with the oracular and the histrionic while seeming to temper them with irony and afterthought. The playful capacities of estrangement are perhaps most apparent in the further reaches of Gallagher's diction: "Dear ones, in those days it was otherwise"; "Denial, O my Senators, / takes a random shape." Less playful and more worrisome tonally are the estrangements of syntax: "he knew something he couldn't know / as only himself, something not to be told again / even by writing down the doing / of it"; "She was brought up manly for a woman / to dread the tender word." Part of the intention here seems to be a kind of new-forged contract between consciousness and language, perception ingenuously reinventing the wheel of the sentence. But the record of consciousness thus produced too often seems to be straining after effect.

The most obvious correlate of the dramatized "I" in these poems is a high level of self-consciousness about the transcription of imagination. Rather than equating the landscape made desolate by season and industry with the landscape made desolate by the technologies of war, the poet will write as follows: "Water / standing in yellow grass, leaves, a few / left hanging, tortured so / the words defoliation and napalm occur." She will write: "I appreciate the rains, / their atonements for my neglect." She will write: "I feel a longing / for religion." The self-referential has of late, and for powerful cause, acquired a good deal of cachet in a multitude of written genres, anthropology and literary theory prominent among them. Self-reference may be used in poetry, as in these more discursive modes, to subvert or circumscribe self-regard. In Gallagher's poetry it does the opposite.

The dramatized self in these poems bears the burden of moral consciousness, of course, mapping the cultural terrain by gestures of empathy (toward a Russian poet, toward celebrants at an Irish wedding) and repugnance (toward the agents of privilege and neocolonialism in impoverished Brazil). The central moral fable of Gallagher's four books is the fable of class, and foothold here is precarious. The plot, quite common in American poetry during the last forty years, is one of escape from the working class to the writing class and the privileges of reflection. "Is that / what you do for a living?" asks a black porter of the poet on a train. "You're lucky." The poet's honorable response is to make of the poem "a morality," "a living" in more than the economic sense. Nevertheless, the luck that divides her from the lives of her parents and siblings while preserving that other life as poetic subject and the commonly coded ground of poetic "authenticity" is luck with a cutting edge. Such luck tends, for one thing, to complicate virtue with virtue's spoils. When the poet, whose motive and range of sympathies derive in part from early constraint, writes a poem about visiting Brazil, she and her famous companion are guests of the lecture circuit; they stay at a luxury hotel. Carolyn Forché, in her strategic second book, tackled head on this bifurcation of experience and the related circle of self-promotion. In a preemptive gesture of simultaneous boast and confession, Forché wrote, "If you read this poem, write to me. / I have been to Paris since we parted," this to a childhood friend who never got out, who lives with her broken husband in a trailer near Detroit. Gallagher means, I think, to explicate the same double bind, but her equipment is cruder. In the title poem of her new collection, Gallagher drives with her brother through the mill town of their childhood in "Ray's Mercedes." Less willing than Forché to discredit the boast herself, Gallagher lets the boast discredit her.

The wages of self-consciousness are mixed. Much to the credit of *Amplitude,* its poems make of memory a dialectical movement, framed and double-framed by the mortal distance of gain and loss. The moving collection of poems to the poet's father, to her mother, to her brothers dead and alive, find in the heart's good chambers and in the filiations of domestic love plenty of room to accommodate mere contradiction (see, for instance, the genial tough-mindedness of "Cougar Meat"). The disciplined nay-sayings of "Message for the Sinecurist" and "The Story of a Citizen" lend counterpoint and sinew to the varied affirmations of "Redwing," "Small Garden Near a Field," "Bonfire," and a host of other poems. And among the other attractions of this volume, there are poems—"Black Silk" from *Willingly* and "His Shining Helmet: Its Horsehair Crest" among the *New Poems*—whose emotional and material economies are shapeliness itself.

Gerald Stern, *Lovesick*

Our leaders have taken to invoking what they call our "Judeo-Christian" heritage, drawing the bland, assimilated face of nationalism over the contestatory agendas of faith and history and contemporary political debate. Nevermind the foreign and domestic policies implicit in Judeo-Christianity, thus invoked; never mind the large populations and many varieties of religious conviction, American too, excluded by the Judeo-Christian embrace. The hyphenated term itself translates into a happy syncretism one of the great colonial annexations of human history, the annexation that made the Hebrew testament "old."

Gerald Stern, the poet personal, the loafer, the celebrant, the kvetch, corrects for the blandness of officialdom with wit and rue, traces the fault lines in the Jewish and Christian portions of our common life, says Kaddish for Western Civ., finds solace in the Lamb of God, rehearses the Diaspora in little space. In the uneasy conflation of Judeo-Christianity Stern locates a thousand contradictions and absurdities, much subterfuge, the sweet trace of human hope. Having moved to the Protestant Midwest, for instance, the Jewish poet hears the hymns of Luther in the very birdsong and looks for cover, the double cover of conciliation ("a friend of all the Anabaptists, a friend / of all the Luther-ans . . . I was good and careful") and imaginative retreat (to the normative, urban "thicket": "Dutch on one side, American Sioux on the other, / Puerto Rican and Bronx Hasidic inside"). No false squeamishness or scruple here. The survivor is an oppor-tunist, trafficking in the second-hand and pirated articles of faith, crossing ethnic and sacramental lines to raid the nearest image bank. Afflicted by a bad back, Stern looks for comfort and example to the butchered sacrifice, contriving in his pain a par-odic *imitatio Christi* ("I Sometimes Think of the Lamb"). Wan-dering through the airports of America, whose poets all wish to be rock stars or athletes, whose poets seek authenticity in pain, having discovered their audience to be smaller than that of rock stars and athletes, Stern addresses the ecumenical confraternity (this world is male) of wandering poets. "Ah brother Levine and brother Stanley Plumly," he moans, "brother Ignatow, oh br'er / Bly": the stops on the reading tour are stations of the cross; the crown of laurel is a crown of thorns ("Arranging a Thorn"). In an age whose recrudescent fundamentalisms are inimical to humor in the public domain, Stern uses the patchwork vest-ments of religion to costume a social comedy of male bonding and self-pity.

The comedy, like all good comedy, is serious business. In "Stolen Face," Stern searches for soul mates among the artifac-tual records of cultural displacement: in a twelfth-century face of stone, pillaged from its original site and built into an arch in a public piazza in Lucca; in the painted face of Christ, revised and canceled and reconstructed for the five hundred years sur-veyed in an art book; in the mirrored face of the tourist/poet, its lineaments partly obscured by age, the aging partly obscured by darkness. "I am the one from Asbury Park, I am / the one from New Orleans, the one from France, / the one from Philadelphia. I believe / the Jews of Russia came afrom Asia, but the Jews / of Poland came from Spain and Africa." (*Afrom:* the typesetter's unchecked error briefly simulates a homesick writer's wistful rendition of Italian-American; in either guise the word is another tag-end of cultural transmission.) In the stolen face at the base of the arch, mirrored and opposed by its brother on the other side; in the face of Jesus, stolen from the Hebrews and made Christian; in the Asia, Spain, and Africa that make his own mixed blood, Stern reads a history of the licensed Jew. Here is the moneylender, the rag-man, the ghetto-dweller-on-sufferance, Italy's commodity of strangers:

> I listen. I learned that idleness
> from Moses. . . . I show him
> my sack of old clothes, he likes that, I show him my permits
> to trade with the East, I show him my medicines—
> I am allowed to practice—I show him my bills
> of lading—they are just old receipts but he is
> impressed. I sit on the hood to hear his sermon—
> ah, I will convert, believe me.

Educated in the bloody schoolroom of "tolerance," the Jew cultivates a strategic *otium,* acquired "from Moses." Harbored in that marginal terrain where strangers are familiars, the poet resorts to silence, exile, and cunning.

In a poem of retrospection ("Knowledge Forwards and Backwards"), Stern makes clear that the estate of licensed strangeness is not the exclusive heritage of Jews, is as much a metaphysical as an ethnic or a literary phenomenon. "We were not yet assimilated," he says of himself and another child; "nothing fit us, our shoes were rotten; it takes / time to adjust to our lives." The old country is childhood itself, or that dark place before childhood, toward which we are moving again. Assimilation is thus the cultivated amnesia and euphemism of daily life or, more disturbingly, the accommodation of darkness to pleasure. In "The Dog," the poet, a "lover of dead things" with pencil in hand, takes road kill for his muse and for his model in the art of pleasing. "I have given / my life for this," says the dead dog by the side of the road; "I have exchanged my wildness . . . / I wait for the cookie, I snap my teeth— / as you have taught me, oh distant and brilliant and lonely." It is the job of the poet, as of any good domestic animal, to die before us, to remind us of the unassimilable, to be just that portion of strangeness that will flatter our regard.

Curator of death, Stern devotes much space to obsessive documentation of the body natural, its postures of supplication and joy, its aches, its moans, its ripeness for the worm of love and the worm of death; thus *Lovesick,* the title of his book. In Stern's songs of praise, the spontaneous orisons of Adam filter down through the indignities of tendon and bone: "If I can bend down I'll touch / my forehead to some stone." In Stern's vision of the afterlife, the dead still suffer and savor the shuffle of mortal constraint: "If only we had wrapped him in his sheet / so he could be prepared; there is such horror / standing before Persephone with a suit on, / the name of the manufacturer in the lining, / the pants too short, or too long" ("Bob Summers' Body"). No wonder Orpheus haunts these poems: the poet finds him among the *O*'s in the card catalogue ("I Am in Love"); the poet hears Orfeo on the radio ("No Longer Terror"); the poet, "who saw the dead and knew the music," searches for a woman in the underworld, which turns out to be Newark ("Neither English nor Spanish"). The mythic slur on urban New Jersey is typical of tone in this volume, where mortal fear and mortal laughter are deeply intertwined. Orpheus's song once made the Furies weep. But back in the world, in Gerald Stern's world, it conveys its tale of death by submitting, beautifully, humanly, to transience. Scribbled on a yellow tablet, folded in a wallet, the song is "broken words . . . / as if a moth were struggling out of the leather, / half caught between the money and the poetry, / little white one in the ravaged world."

Philip Levine, *A Walk with Tom Jefferson*

New York, Detroit, Fresno, Medford: from a shifting home front, the poet at sixty files his report on "God's Concern / for America." The evidence is not such as to make the poet sanguine. The walls that keep the darkness out are everywhere paper-thin. The news from above is mostly of ourselves: the autumnal sunset brilliant with pollutants, "all the earth we've pumped / into the sky," makes a pageant of doom from the by-products of human hope and industry ("A Walk with Tom Jefferson"). In Fresno, just this side of the fault line, the poet dreams the end of the world ("Waking in March"). The news arrives, bad joke that it is, from the glow above Los Angeles, and the poet can do no more than "go from bed / to bed bowing to the small damp heads / of my sons." Outside the dream, the children have long since left home, but every parent knows those rounds by heart, knows the fault line panic opens beside the beds and their sweet burdens. The children have fallen asleep, imagining that it is safe to do so; the parent, standing for safety, knows that safety is illusion. Who's in charge here?

> If I told you that the old woman
> named Ida Bellow was shot to death
> for no more than $5 and that a baby
> of eighteen months saw it all from
> where she wakened on the same bed
> but can't tell because she can't speak
> you'd say I was making it up
>
> ("These Streets")

While America goes to the dogs, the poet with America stuck in his throat rehearses the lessons of his American masters, of Stevens and Whitman ("I Sing the Body Electric"), of Williams ("A Theory of Prosody"), of the carping Yvor Winters ("28"). Levine writes, as the good ones do, to save his life. He also writes a revisionist aesthetic of Decline and Fall, retrieving poetry from frontier bravado ("Rexroth / reminiscing on a Berkeley FM station in the voice / God uses to lecture Jesus Christ"). To Whitman's triumphant corporeal embrace, to Stevens's pungent oranges and extended wings, Levine replies with the echoing actuarials of Hartford on a Sunday morning ("In my black rain coat I go back / out into the gray morning and dare / the cars on North Indemnity Boulevard / to hit me, but no one wants trouble / at this hour"). To Williams's manifesto on the modernist poetic line ("As the cat / climbed over / the top of / the jamcloset"), Levine replies with feline Nellie, who "would sit behind me / as I wrote" and paw at the hand that extended a line too far. "The first / time she drew blood I learned / it was poetic to end / a line anywhere to keep her / quiet." To Winters, for whom meter was morality and syntax a hedge against chaos, Levine replies with loopy numerology: the poet at fifty-six traces the numbered highways of America, the enumerated rehearsals of oblivion (fourteen hours of fevered sleep, three close encounters with death), and the domestic plenum (two opposing families of five) back to himself at twenty-eight, just half the age of the century, half the age of his newfound mentor (Winters in Los Altos), half the age of the older self who writes this poem.

Winters titled his collected prose *In Defense of Reason*. Levine's bittersweet critique of reason records the patent incapacity of form to structure meaning, all the while making meaning of vaporous coincidence.

Escaping the dead end of swing-shift Detroit for sumptuous California, the artist as a young man delivered himself into the hands of one who, all but forgotten among younger writers now, was a name to conjure with in the middle decades of the twentieth century: a poet who came to believe that free verse led to madness, a critic who represented the far right fringe of the canon police, a teacher, bless him, who fostered most passionately those protegés most certain to defect. While Winters presided in the hills of Los Altos and the gentlemen's club of Stanford, the young Levine kept house with two kids and a pregnant wife in East Palo Alto, Stanford's shadow ghetto, an unincorporated stretch of cinder block and prefab for the un- and the underemployed. For the apprentice poet, California's royal way—El Camino Real—was a divider strip between the good life and real life, a place for poaching lilacs. The poaching has stood him in good stead, evolving a poetry whose range of consciousness and conscience, whose capacity for anger and debunking and sweet recuperation lends heart to the embattled republic, or to those of its citizens with leisure to read.

In the title poem of his new book, Levine takes a mentor of another sort. Brought up from Alabama on the dream of five dollars a day, Tom Jefferson, grown old now, tends a garden in the gutted Promised Land, "Between the freeway / and the gray conning towers / of the ballpark" in postindustrial Detroit. Having lost his youth to the auto plant and his son to Korea, Tom Jefferson quotes Scripture and pushes a shopping cart through abandoned lots. Tom Jefferson "is a believer. / You can't plant winter vegetables / if you aren't." Tom Jefferson takes his name from the slave-holding theorist of liberty and "property," revised to the pursuit of happiness. Walking with Tom Jefferson, Levine recalls his own first part in capitalism's long last coma:

> when I worked nights
>   on the milling machines
>   at Cadillac transmission,
>   another kid just up

    from West Virginia asked me
         what was we making,
    and I answered, I'm making
         2.25 an hour,
    don't know what you're
         making, and he had
    to correct me, gently, what was
         we making out of
    this here metal, and I didn't know.

What he ultimately made, of course, was work of another sort. The thirteen bound volumes of that work to date, remarkable intersections of private memory and political fable, will not, unaided, cure what ails us. But in an age more notable for overflowing landfills than for neighborhood renewal, it is much to make poems that heal the breach between ignorance and understanding, labor and wage.

11

The Sower against Gardens

The gods, that mortal beauty chase,
Still in a tree did end their race.
                                    —Andrew Marvell

Louise Glück is one of those enviable poets whose powers and
distinction emerged early and were early recognized. Her work
has been justly admired and justly influential, as only work of
the very first order can be: work so impeccably itself that it alters
the landscape in which others write while at the same time dis-
couraging (and dooming) the ordinary homage of direct imita-
tion. In 1992 Glück published a sixth book and in 1996 a sev-
enth, which, in their sustained engagement with inherited fable
and inherited form, in their simultaneously witty and deadly se-
rious subversions, constitute a deepening so remarkable that it
amounts to a new departure. These books are unlike one an-
other in any number of outward dispositions, but they share a
common intellectual purchase; they are two poles of a single
project.

1. Like Me

The Wild Iris makes its entrance late in the life of a tradition and
its self-wrought woes: the moral and aesthetic dilemmas of sen-
timental projection, the metaphysical dilemma of solitude (if the
others with whom I am in dialogue are merely the projections
of self, I am alone in the world, and, worse, the world has been
lost on me). The poet plants herself in a garden and dares its
other Creator to join her. The poet construes her garden to be

First published in *The Kenyon Review* N.S. 23, no. 1 (winter 2001): 115–33.

an anthropomorphic thicket and a series of moral exempla. The poet ventriloquizes all the voices—floral, human, transcendent—in a family quarrel about love and sustenance. With equal portions of bravura and self-deprecation, wit and rue, *The Wild Iris* mindfully renders its dilemmas by means of an interwoven series of dramatic monologues. These have, some of them, been published separately (they are poems of great individual beauty), but they are not separable: the book is a single meditation that far exceeds its individual parts.

The monologues are of three sorts: (1) those spoken by a human persona to God, or to that which holds the place of God; (2) those spoken by the botanical inhabitants of the garden cultivated by the human persona; and (3) those spoken by divinity. The poems addressed to God take their titles and their rhetorical premise from the Christian canonical hours (here reduced from seven to two), which mark the daily cycles of prayer. The poems spoken by flowers, groundcover, and one flowering tree take their color and argument from the circumstances of individual species (annuals vs. perennials, shade plants vs. sun plants, single blossoms vs. multiple); excluded from voicing are only those vegetable denizens identified with human "use" or consumption. The God-voiced poems take their titles from the saturating conditions of nature: weather, season, the qualities of wind or light. The poet is clearly aware that her central device, the affective identification that characterizes so large a portion of nature poetry in English, has sometimes borne the stigma of "fallacy," so she incorporates a preemptive ironist:

> The sun shines; by the mailbox, leaves
> Of the divided birch tree folded, pleated like fins.
> Underneath, hollow stems of the white daffodils,
>   Ice Wings, Cantatrice; dark
> leaves of the wild violet. Noah says
> depressives hate the spring, imbalance
> between the inner and the outer world. I make
> another case—being depressed, yes, but in a sense passionately
> attached to the living tree, my body
> actually curled in the split trunk, almost at peace,
>   in the evening rain
> almost able to feel
> sap frothing and rising: Noah says this is

an error of depressives, identifying
with a tree, whereas the happy heart
wanders the garden like a falling leaf, a figure for
the part, not the whole.

("Matins," 2)

If we are paying attention, we can discern the season before
Noah names it: daffodils are a spring flower; the leaves of the
birch tree are as yet unfolded. But the foreboding that attaches
to the season is entirely inexplicit until Noah is made to com-
ment upon it and, commenting, to deflate it. "Entirely" is per-
haps misleading. In situ, in the full *Wild Iris,* some portion of
foreboding inevitably infects this poem by way of the poem that
immediately precedes it. In that previous poem, which is also the
title poem, the awakening rendered in the voice of an iris is a
transition of stirring beauty ("from the center of my life came /
a great fountain, deep blue / shadows on azure seawater") and
intractable pain ("It is terrible to survive / as consciousness /
buried in the dark earth"). But that which is metaphysical in
"The Wild Iris" and mythic in the mind of the "Matins" speaker
(notice her partial invocation of Daphne) is in Noah's breezy
analysis a thing considerably more banal. Instead of ontology,
the garden's resident ironist discerns psychology; instead of
tragic insight, the symptomatic "presentation" of temperament
or disease. This witty, transient pathologizing of point of view
produces a marvelous mobility of tone, a mobility manifest in
local instances of Glück's earlier work but never so richly devel-
oped as in the present volume. And never so strategically impor-
tant. By anticipating and incorporating the skeptical reader, by
fashioning the poetic sequence as a dialogue with disbelief, the
speaker procures considerable license for her extravagant im-
personations: of violets, of witchgrass, of Eve in the Garden, nay,
of God. We find early on that we will grant this speaker any num-
ber of investigations-by-means-of-likeness. And why? Because we
like her.

God and the flowers speak with the voice of the human; the
human writer has no other voice to give them. The flowers sense,
or describe sensation, in unabashedly human terms: "I feel it /
glinting through the leaves," says the shaded vine, "like someone
hitting the side of a glass with a metal spoon" ("Lamium"). They

measure aptitude by contrast or analogy with human aptitude: "Things / that can't move," says the rooted tree, "learn to see; I do not need / to chase you through / the garden" ("The Hawthorne Tree"); "I am not like you," says the rose, "I have only / my body for a voice" ("The White Rose"). God speaks in the voice of an earthly parent who has reached the end of his tether: "How can I help you when you all want / different things" ("Midsummer"); "Do you suppose I care / if you speak to one another?" ("April"). God explains himself by analogy and contradistinction to the human: "I am not like you in this, / I have no release in another body" ("End of Summer"). God, like his creatures, assumes the simplifying contours of the familial: "You were like very young children, / always waiting for a story. . . . / I was tired of telling stories" ("Retreating Light").

But likeness marks an irreparable chasm as well:

> So I gave you the pencil and paper.
> I gave you pens made of reeds
> I had gathered myself, afternoons in the dense meadows.
> I told you, write your own story.
> . . . .
> Then I realized you couldn't think
> with any real boldness or passion;
> you hadn't had your own lives yet,
> your own tragedies.
> So I gave you lives, I gave you tragedies,
> because apparently tools alone weren't enough.
>
> You will never know how deeply
> it pleases me to see you sitting there
> like independent beings.
>
> ("Retreating Light")

That *like* is ice to the heart. Those who achieve authentic independence require no *like*.

Shadowing this book is the troubling possibility, indeed, the certain knowledge, that its analogies are false or partial. "Whatever you hoped," says God in the voice of the wind, "you will not find yourselves in the garden, / among the growing plants. / Your lives are not circular like theirs" ("Retreating Wind"). Worse yet from the poet's perspective, her analogies may be forced: "If this were not a poem but / an actual garden," one skeptical interlocutor opines, "then / the red rose would be required to resemble nothing else, neither / another flower nor / the shadowy heart" ("Song"). Our Renaissance forebears had a term for the clothing of divinity in earthly garments: they called this process *accommodation*. Because we are weak, because we cannot behold divinity face to face, God "accommodates" himself to our limits, agreeing to be known by elements available to human sense. These measures, however, are imperfect and interim:

> I've submitted to your preferences, observing patiently
> the things you love, speaking
>
> through vehicles only, in
> details of earth, as you prefer,
>
> tendrils
> of blue clematis, light
>
> of early evening—
> you would never accept
>
> a voice like mine, indifferent
> to the objects you busily name,
>
> your mouths
> small circles of awe—
>
> And all this time
> I indulged your limitation.
>
> ("Clear Morning")

Glück's couplets do not in any straightforward sense coincide with the divisions of dialogue, but they do, subtly, remind us that accommodation is a two-part contract. God's patience is not infinite: "I cannot go on / restricting myself to images // because you think it is your right / to dispute my meaning" ("Clear Morning"). In order to grant his creatures an interim meeting place, the Creator agrees to interim diminishment. But this delicate contract breaks down the minute it is presumed upon:

> You were not intended
> to be unique. You were
> my embodiment, all diversity

> not what you think you see
> searching the bright sky over the field,
> your incidental souls
> fixed like telescopes on some
> enlargement of yourselves—
>
> ("Midsummer")

Do not flatter yourselves, the Creator warns. Despite what you imagine, what I allow you for a time to imagine, I am not like you.

2. We

And you are plural. You are mere repetitive examples, as the crowd beneath your feet can witness:

> Not I, you idiot, not self, but we, we—waves
> of sky blue like
> a critique of heaven: why
> do you treasure your voice
> when to be one thing
> is to be next to nothing?
> Why do you look up? To hear
> an echo like the voice
> of god?
>
> ("Scilla")

The plural pronoun is a reproach to vanity, and in *The Wild Iris* it issues not only from below but from above as well, and in the harsher second person:

> You wanted to be born; I let you be born.
> When has my grief ever gotten
> in the way of your pleasure?
>
> Plunging ahead . . .
> as though you were some new thing, wanting
> to express yourselves . . .
>
> never thinking
> this would cost you anything,
> never imagining the sound of my voice
> as anything but part of you—
>
> ("End of Winter")

The accusatory mode is one the human persona can adopt as well. "How can I live / in colonies, as you prefer," she asks, "if you impose / a quarantine of affliction, dividing me / from healthy members of / my own tribe" ("Matins," 26). This counter-complaint, with its foundational recourse to a singular self, is all the more credible for missing the point. But the leverage inherent in the first-person plural has not been entirely lost on the human speaker; she too can manipulate the moral advantage in numbers when she will: "Unreachable father, when we were first / exiled from heaven, you made / a replica, a place in one sense / different from heaven, being / designed to teach a lesson" ("Matins," 3). In one sense, the speaker's imperturbable assumptions about didactic function are simply another manifestation of self-regard: the garden cannot simply be; the garden must mean; it was made *for me.* And though the speaker describes an affliction shared with others, or one particular other, of her kind, the shared aptitude appears to be for solitude: "Left alone, / we exhausted each other" ("Matins," 3). What lifts these passages above the common run of vanity is the ground of knowing they describe: "We never thought of you / whom we were learning to worship. / We merely knew it wasn't human nature to love / only what returns love" ("Matins," 3). In *The Wild Iris,* as in its dominant line of lyric forebears, unrequited longing is the constitutive feature of consciousness. The garden is a sign because it is redolent with absence. The sharers in the garden come to know themselves by knowing that something is missing; their very failure to sustain one another is part of the message.

Given all this absence, what may we infer about the Maker? He has absconded. His voice is "the persistent echoing / in all sound that means good-bye, good-bye— / the one continuous line / that binds us to each other" ("End of Winter"). The *we* that includes deity is a *we* shot through with departure, so in his leaving, the deity has left us one another, another *we.* And how have we made use of this solace?

> *No one's despair is like my despair—*
>
> You have no place in this garden
> thinking such things, producing
> the tiresome outward signs; the man
> pointedly weeding an entire forest,

the woman limping, refusing to change clothes
or wash her hair.

Do you suppose I care
if you speak to one another?
But I mean you to know
I expected better of two creatures
who were given minds: if not
that you would actually care for each other
at least that you would understand
grief is distributed
between you, among all your kind, for me
to know you, as deep blue
marks the wild scilla, white
the wood violet.

("April")

The irritable reaching after uniqueness ("No one's despair is like my despair") has taken its toll on human community. Despair has become for the couple in the garden a competitive pastime. But behind the orthodox proposition that despair is a species of pride, self-made and self-sustained, lies a yet more chilling possibility: what if we are on to the truth in spite of ourselves? What if grief is indeed our only claim to distinction? When the biblical faithful are forced to consider that their ends may not be coincident with the ends of the Creator, they have generally contrived to find this difference reassuring: God knows better; God makes us suffer for our own good. But what if God doesn't know better at all? Or what if his knowing doesn't have much to do with us? What if, except for our suffering, God could not tell us apart?

The distributed personae of *The Wild Iris* think through to the other side of this all-but-unthinkable proposition from time to time, think beyond the obvious panic such a proposition induces, and address deity as another of the vulnerable species of creation:

—I am ashamed
at what I thought you were,
distant from us, regarding us
as an experiment . . .
        . . . Dear friend,

> dear trembling partner, what
> surprises you most in what you feel,
> earth's radiance or your own delight?
>
> ("Matins," 31)

This is not the voice of first, or naive, intimacy, not the voice of the child who takes for granted that the parent is near, but the voice of willed, or revisionist, intimacy, the voice of the adult who has wearied of blame. It is a voice that may be adopted not only by the privileged species for whom the garden was created but also, and with equal eloquence, by the garden's humblest residents:

> Because in our world
> something is always hidden,
> small and white,
> small and what you call
> pure, we do not grieve
> as you grieve, dear
> suffering master; you
> are no more lost
> than we are, under
> the hawthorn tree, the hawthorn holding
> balanced trays of pearls: what
> has brought you among us
> who would teach you, though
> you kneel and weep,
> clasping your great hands,
> in all your greatness knowing
> nothing of the soul's nature,
> which is never to die: poor sad god,
> either you never have one
> or you never lose one.
>
> ("Violets")

Nowhere in this limpid book does its triangular logic emerge with greater resonance. The human addresses God for the most part; the flowers and God address the human. And sometimes, to the flowers, the human appears in the guise of God, as flawed as the God to whom humans turn. But where is the human in "Violets"? Between "our world" and "your great hands," the human may be present, for once, chiefly by omission. And the posited soul: how is it that the violets know it? Do they have a soul? Does God? Does one have to have a soul in order to know the nature of the soul? Or does one know the nature of the soul only from the outside, only by being without one? Are we to imagine that the poor sad god in the garden grieves at being without a soul? Or does he grieve because he is unable to be rid of the soul? The only point on which the violets appear to speak unambiguously, a point quite devastating enough, is that grieving will not *make* a soul.

We three then: the two in dialogue and the one just beyond the bounds of dialogue, in whom the dialogue is grounded. The triangular manipulation of presence is as old as the lyric itself. He who sits beside you, writes Sappho. She that hath you, Shakespeare writes. Jealousy stands for but also masks a more frightening possibility. "Much / has passed between us," writes Glück; "or / was it always only / on the one side?" ("Matins," 13).

3. Reciprocal

The spectral possibility that gives lyric its urgency is not that the beloved isn't listening, but that the beloved doesn't exist. Prayer takes place at the edge of a similar abyss:

> Once I believed in you; I planted a fig tree.
> Here, in Vermont, country
> of no summer. It was a test: if the tree lived,
> it would mean you existed.
>
> By this logic, you do not exist. Or you exist
> exclusively in warmer climates,
> in fervent Sicily and Mexico and California,
> where are grown the unimaginable
> apricot and fragile peach. Perhaps
> they see your face in Sicily; here, we barely see
> the hem of your garment. I have to discipline myself
> to share with John and Noah the tomato crop.
> ("Vespers," 36)

The poet's logic here is that of clever blackmail. God won't show? Perhaps he can be taunted into breaking cover. The speaker plants a fig tree, or the story of a fig tree, as a dare. When the fig tree predictably dies, the dare modulates to witty demotion. Are you not here, Father? Perhaps you are somewhere else? Or perhaps you are littler than we thought. To propose that God might "exist exclusively in warmer climates" is to bait a withholding deity: it goes without saying that God can be no God unless he is everywhere at once. Or does it? Perhaps the absurdity cuts both ways. Perhaps comedic gesture throws into relief the deep peculiarity of an all-or-nothing system that is premised on "jealousy." A jealous God gets the jealous children ("I have to discipline myself," etc.) he deserves.

> If there is justice in some other world, those
> like myself, whom nature forces
> into lives of abstinence, should get
> the lion's share of all things, all
> objects of hunger, greed being
> praise of you. And no one praises
> more intensely than I, with more
> painfully checked desire, or more deserves
> to sit at your right hand, if it exists, partaking
> of the perishable, the immortal fig,
> which does not travel.
>
> ("Vespers," 36)

Gospel has promised that the poor shall possess the kingdom of heaven, and the poet wants her share, "the lion's share," of this compensatory promotion. Far from admitting greed as grounds for penance, she brazenly advances greed as the badge of special comprehension and thus of special desert. If God has bounty to dispense, then perhaps, like other patrons, he may be bribed. Praise is the coinage of patronage, whose darker side is *if*. "If there is justice in some other world": the conditional clause says justice in the present world has fallen short. "If it exists": the conditional clause insinuates that part of the power, and part of the power to judge, resides with the believer. If the Father, in order to exist, requires our faith as we require his bounty, we may have found the key to reciprocal consent. But lest the contract prove too dry, the poet does not stop here, does not pause too long to congratulate herself for unmasking the circular structure of vested interest. She returns instead to the object that passes between the master and the lovers in the garden, that makes the longing palpable, or nearly so: the promised, the withheld, the here-and-absent fig.

For the lover is a gardener too:

> In your extended absence, you permit me
> use of earth, anticipating
> some return on investment.

("Vespers," 37)

This gardener glances obliquely at the parable of the talents (see Matthew 25; see Milton's nineteenth sonnet). It is a useful parable, invoking spiritual and mercenary economies in unseemly proximity. Unseemliness prompts resistence, a common heuristic device. It also prompts reproach:

> I must report
> failure in my assignment, principally
> regarding the tomato plants.

("Vespers," 37)

Adopting the disconsonant diction of spreadsheet and quarterly report, the gardener achieves a wicked deadpan, fair warning that she does not intend to shoulder the failure alone:

> I think I should not be encouraged to grow
> tomatoes. Or, if I am, you should withhold
> the heavy rains, the cold nights that come
> so often here, while other regions get
> twelve weeks of summer

("Vespers," 37)

The multiplying indecorums now include domestic comedy. The disgruntled dependent resourcefully finds that she is not to blame after all, that someone else has caused her fault, someone whose crime is the misapportionment of original love. And then, apparent concession: "All this / belongs to you." But the concession is quickly withdrawn:

> All this
> belongs to you: on the other hand,
> I planted the seeds, I watched the first shoots

like wings tearing the soil, and it was my heart
broken by the blight, the black spot so quickly
multiplying in the rows. I doubt
you have a heart, in our understanding of
that term. You who do not discriminate
between the dead and the living, who are, in consequence,
immune to foreshadowing, you may not know
how much terror we bear, the spotted leaf,
the red leaves of the maple falling
even in August, in early darkness: I am responsible
for these vines.

("Vespers," 37)

The hilarious, instantaneous taking back of that which was fleet-
ingly granted—God's proprietary interest in creation—begins
in petulance: mine, says the poet; the suffering is mine. But
petulance expands to a countercharge—you have no heart—
that bit by bit accumulates plausibility. God's loftier perspective,
his comprehensive vision, begins to look like insufficiency. For
comprehensiveness is by its very nature incapable of something
too, incapable of "foreshadowing," of temporal habitation, of
partialness and partiality, the realms of feeling possessed by
those who are subject to time. Unfolding these realms, the
human voice becomes tutelary, makes concession to the newly
contemplated incapacities of deity: "You may not know."

And then the inventory of terror: the spotted leaf, the falling
leaf, the early darkness. And, signaled by the colon, the syllo-
gistic revelation: I am the only one left to be responsible. The
line is not merely syllogistic, of course. Spoken within the pa-
rameters of apostrophic address, and spoken to one who might
have been assumed to be responsible himself, it is a reprimand:
unlike you, I take my responsibilities to heart. The reprimand
is also a piece of gamesmanship, another in the series of rhetor-
ical moves designed to flush God out. By what standard may we
judge its success? God has not, we must confess, been coerced
into unambiguous manifestation. On the other hand, the game
has not quite stalled. For, even as the speaker makes her sinu-
ous case for self, something beyond the self—a "we" who bear
the terror, the vines—has claimed the self's attention. This may
be small. It is certainly strategic. But even in the momentary,
the strategic assumption of responsibility, the self accrues a new

degree of moral dignity. This moment may be as close as God will come.

In poem after poem, *The Wild Iris* delineates a reciprocal drawing out of spirit. This is not to say it is a sanguine book:

> Sometimes a man or woman forces his despair
> on another person, which is called
> baring the heart, alternatively, baring the soul—
> meaning for this moment they acquired souls—
>
> ("Love in Moonlight")

Moonlight is reflected light, light "taken from another source," and love in this light a kind of violent seizing, or theft. The God who may or may not exist may take his logic from moonlight or love or, failing that, from parables. "You are perhaps training me to be / responsive to the slightest brightening," the poet ventures. "Or, like the poets, / are you stimulated by despair?" ("Vespers," 43). The poet takes a walk at sunset in the company of her despair. And in helpless arousal or deliberate grace, in one of two contrary modes, the God she refuses to look for appears:

>   As you anticipated,
> I did not look up. So you came down to me:
> at my feet, not the wax
> leaves of the wild blueberry but your fiery self, a whole
> pasture of fire, and beyond, the red sun neither falling
>   nor rising—
> I was not a child; I could take advantage of illusions.
>
> ("Vespers," 43)

This final resolution might be epigraph to the entire book of the garden.

4. Domestic

The domestic comedy that offers counterpoint to metaphysical debate in *The Wild Iris* assumes center stage in *Meadowlands,* the book of poems Glück published four years later. In this new book, the garden has given way to landscape of a different sort: the grasslands behind a childhood home on Long Island or surrounding the home of a twenty-year marriage in Vermont, the grasslands long buried beneath a football stadium in industrial New Jersey. Glück's subject has long been the zero-sum game of the nuclear family (even when she grants a place to grandparents, aunts, and a sister's children, they are merely the reiterative instances of nuclear entrapment). The wit and the paradox, the razor-edge renderings of human motivation and human stalemate have been in place for decades. But now they are fresher, deeper than ever before. What has moved the project forward so dramatically is a structural insight: the deployment of inherited patterns (devotional hours, growing season, garden epic, voyage epic, scripts for different voices) on a book-length scale. Like *The Wild Iris, Meadowlands* has been constructed as a single argument, internally cross-referenced, dramatically unified. Its story is the breakdown of a marriage, and its template is Homeric.

What has the marriage in *Meadowlands* to do with the story of Odysseus and Penelope? Its time span is roughly twenty years, divided into two decade-long segments, one of them "happy." Its measure is roughly the span of a young son's growing into manhood, and judgment, and ironic commentary. Its outward incidents are driven by a husband's appetite for adventure. Its deeper momentum derives from the tension between excursis and domesticity. But the template yields rich results precisely because its fit is only approximate.

> Little soul, little perpetually undressed one,
> do now as I bid you, climb
> the shelf-like branches of the spruce tree;
> wait at the top, attentive, like
> a sentry or look-out. He will be home soon;
> it behooves you to be
> generous. You have not been completely
> perfect either; with your troublesome body
> you have done things you shouldn't
> discuss in poems. Therefore
> call out to him over the open water, over the bright water
> with your dark song, with your grasping,
> unnatural song—passionate,
> like Maria Callas. Who
> wouldn't want you? Whose most demonic appetite

could you possibly fail to answer? Soon
he will return from wherever he goes in the meantime,
suntanned from his time away, wanting
his grilled chicken. Ah, you must greet him,
you must shake the boughs of the tree
to get his attention,
but carefully, carefully, lest
his beautiful face be marred
by too many falling needles.

("Penelope's Song")

If the second Homeric epic has held enduring appeal for female narrators, this surely has something to do with Penelope's leveraged position in a complex economy of desire. The human heroines of the *Iliad* are essentially single-function figures, the bearers of prophecy, grief, beauty, and fidelity in a world whose primary contests—erotic, political, martial—are waged by men. But Penelope's position is sustained by ambiguities as rich as those that sustain Achilles. She weaves a shroud for a patriarch who is not yet dead; she rules a royal household, albeit in a compromised and declining state, during the prolonged absence of her husband and the minority of her son; she entertains a populous band of suitors whose extended address makes her uniquely immune to the erosions of age. Penelope has every reason to delay, and the reader has every reason to lodge in her vicinity. Her cup is never empty, her position ever summary: wife, mother, queen, perpetual subject of desire. If the quality of that desire is somewhat clouded by a husband's waywardness and the suitors' greed and boorishness, its breadth and duration are nevertheless the stuff of fantasy. Finally, crucially, Penelope's composite position makes her a center of consciousness, something to which not even the paragon Helen may aspire.

"But carefully, carefully, lest / his beautiful face be marred / by too many falling needles." The poet wears her mythic trappings lightly when it suits her: the frank anachronisms of Maria Callas and grilled chicken are fair indicators. The falling needles of a pine tree may be a poem's only, oblique allusion to the heroine's clothworking artistry, which signifies retirement (the upstairs loom) and an aptitude for aggression (some damage to the hero's face). The framework of *Meadowlands* will open to admit any number of irreverent intrusions from late in the second millenium: a dishwasher, a purple bathing suit, the neighbors' klezmer band, a resolute vernacular. Nor are the book's mythic templates exclusively Homeric: one poem draws its title and its premise (the ordinary miracle of marriage) from the wedding at Cana, one is addressed to the serpent of Genesis, several make of birds and beasts and flowering plants a built-to-purpose parable. Narrative foundations are overlapping and distillate: the wife divides her perspective among several alter egos, several island wives, including her chief rival, Circe. The husband's reiterated departure seems sometimes to be his departure from the modern marriage, sometimes the infidelities that prepare for that departure, sometimes Odysseus's departure for Troy, sometimes his serial departures on the homeward trip to Ithaca, sometimes the shadowy final departure rehearsed in epic continuations like the *Inferno* or the lost *Telegonia*.[1]

The great advantage of broad outline is its suppleness, its freedom from clutter.

> The Greeks are sitting on the beach
> wondering what to do when the war ends. No one
> wants to go home, back
> to that bony island; everyone wants a little more
> of what there is in Troy, more
> life on the edge, that sense of every day as being
> packed with surprises. But how to explain this
> to the ones at home to whom
> fighting a war is a plausible
> excuse for absence, whereas
> exploring one's capacity for diversion
> is not.
>
> ("Parable of the Hostages")

This freedom from clutter is a rhetorical talent shared by Telemachus, whose earlier incarnation was as Noah in *The Wild Iris*. Telemachus has learned that ironists need never be out of work:

> When I was a child looking
> at my parents' lives, you know
> what I thought? I thought
> heartbreaking. Now I think
> heartbreaking, but also

insane. Also
very funny.

("Telemachus' Detachment")

The domestic quarrel, with its soul-destroying pettiness and convolution, would seem to be inimical to lyric poetry. One of the great technical triumphs of *Meadowlands* is to have found a form in which the soul-destroying can be transmuted to the spirit-reviving. The genius is not just in the leaving out, though elision is its indispensable method, but also in the undressed, unwashed leaving in:

> Speak to me, aching heart: what
> ridiculous errand are you inventing for yourself
> weeping in the dark garage
> with your sack of garbage: it is not your job
> to take out the garbage, it is your job
> to empty the dishwasher. You are showing off again.
>
> ("Midnight")

But Glück's finest formal innovation in this volume is reserved for the structure of domestic dialogue. She tracks the wild non sequitur, the sidestep and the feint, the ambush, the afterthought, the timed delay. As in Penelope's weaving, the thread that seemed to have been dropped resurfaces, having meanwhile leant its tensile continuity to the underside of the narrative.

> How could the Giants name
> that place the Meadowlands? It has
> about as much in common with a pasture
> as would the inside of an oven.

> New Jersey
> was rural. They want you
> to remember that.

> Simms
> was not a thug. LT
> was not a thug.

> What I think is we should
> look at our surroundings
> realistically, for what they are
> in the present.

149

> That's what
> I tell you about the house.
>
> No giant
> would talk the way you talk.
> You'd be a nicer person
> if you were a fan of something.
> When you do that with your mouth
> you look like your mother.
>
> You know what they are?
> Kings among men.
>
> > So what king
> > fired Simms?

("Meadowlands 3")

Ten such dialogue poems appear in the course of *Meadowlands,* eleven if one counts, and one should, the epigraph. All are distinguished by the same minimalist annotation—the woman speaking in indented stanzas, the man flush left—and by a handful of recurrent themes. Once the convention and the leitmotifs have established themselves, the poet is free to begin and end in heady, hilarious *medias res:* three bare lines and a single speaker in "Meadowlands 2," another single speaker in "Void." No matter that the partner in speech is silent for the moment: these poems are cast as rejoinders and thus take part in a two-part song. Their workings are *in situ,* inseparable from the tonal and semantic resource of the book. Given the theme of the book, of course, this indissolubility of the whole achieves no little poignance. And greatly to its credit, it achieves delight. The reader is granted the pleasures of an initiate, one who knows the players without a scorecard, and the pleasures of an exuberant pace. No small prize to rescue from the ashes.

5. One

> Let's play choosing music. Favorite form.
>
> Opera.
>
> Favorite work.
>
> Figaro. No. Figaro and Tannhauser. Now
> it's your turn: sing one for me.

(Epigraph)

Mozart's is a comic opera of marriage. Wagner's is a tragic romance, in which the hero philanders and the heroine dies of a broken heart. Sing one, says the hero: make the one tradition comprehensive. Do the different voices, and make them add up to a whole. Sing for me: make me miss you when I am gone.

"A figure for / the part," said Noah in the earlier book. "Not," he said, "the whole" ("Matins," 2). But his subject was the happy heart. Part of the wit that unites these books is their tracing of great epic themes—Milton's in the first instance, Homer's in the second—to their origins in the domestic. By means of this tracing, they continue the logic already inherent in their lofty predecessors. But the latterday garden and the meadowlands share another logic too, a logic more specific to the lyric. They posit conversation in a fertile world: my part, yours, the whole making more than the sum of its parts. And always they hear the conversation breaking down, the answer reduced to echo, the several voices to one. "The beloved doesn't / need to live," says the weaver with equal parts grimness and joy. "The beloved / lives in the head" ("Ithaca").

NOTE

1. The *Telegonia* (sixth century B.C.E.) takes its name from Telegonus, son of Odysseus and Circe. On the structural kinship and durable erotic powers of rival women this lost epic was apparently superb: its plot is said to have included the ultimate marriage of Circe to Telemachus and Penelope to Telegonus, two mothers to two sons. Odysseus had by this time succumbed.

UNDER DISCUSSION
David Lehman, General Editor
Donald Hall, Founding Editor

Volumes in the Under Discussion series collect reviews and essays about individual poets. The series is concerned with contemporary American and English poets about whom the consensus has not yet been formed and the final vote has not been taken. Titles in the series include: